CW00545809

MAXIMUM ADVERSE EXCURSION

WILEY TRADER'S ADVANTAGE SERIES

Maximum Adverse Excursion

ANALYZING PRICE FLUCTUATIONS FOR TRADING MANAGEMENT

JOHN SWEENEY

JOHN WILEY & SONS, INC.
New York • Chichester • Weinheim • Toronto • Singapore • Brisbane

Copyright © 1997 by John Sweeney.
Published by John Wiley & Sons, Inc.

Library of Congress Cataloging-in-Publication Data:

Sweeney, John.
    Maximum adverse excursion : analyzing price fluctuations for
trading management / John Sweeney.
        p.   cm. — (Wiley trader's advantage series)
    Includes index.
    ISBN 0-471-14152-6 (cloth : alk. paper)
    1. Investment analysis—Mathematical models.   2. Securities—
Prices—Mathematical models.   3. Risk management—Mathematical
models.   I. Title.   II. Series.
HG4529.S93   1996
332.64′01′51—dc20   96-29431

10   9   8   7   6   5   4   3   2   1

THE TRADER'S ADVANTAGE SERIES PREFACE

The Trader's Advantage Series is a new concept in publishing for traders and analysts of futures, options, equity, and generally all world economic markets. Books in the series present single ideas with only that background information needed to understand the content. No long introductions, no definitions of the futures contract, clearing house, and order entry: Focused.

The futures and options industry is no longer in its infancy. From its role as an agricultural vehicle it has become the alter ego of the most active world markets. The use of EFPs (exchange for physicals) in currency markets makes the selection of physical or futures markets transparent, in the same way the futures markets evolved into the official pricing vehicle for world grain. With a singe telephone call, a trader or investment manager can hedge a stock portfolio, set a crossrate, perform a swap, or buy the protection of an inflation index. The classic regimes can no longer be clearly separated.

And this is just the beginning. Automated exchanges are penetrating traditional open outcry markets. Even now, from the time the transaction is completed in the pit, everything else is electronic.

"Program trading" is the automated response to the analysis of a computerized ticker tape, and it is just the tip of the inevitable evolutionary process. Soon the executions will be computerized and then we won't be able to call anyone to complain about a fill. Perhaps we won't even have to place an order to get a fill.

Market literature has also evolved. Many of the books written on trading are introductory. Even those intended for more advanced audiences often include a review of contract specifications and market mechanics. There are very few books specifically targeted for the experienced and professional traders and analysts. *The Trader's Advantage Series* changes all that.

This series presents contributions by established professionals and exceptional research analysts. The author's highly specialized talents have been applied primarily to futures, cash, and equity markets but are often generally applicable to price forecasting. Topics in the series include trading systems and individual techniques, but all are a necessary part of the development process that is intrinsic to improving price forecasting and trading.

These works are creative, often state-of-the-art. They offer new techniques, in-depth analysis of current trading methods, or innovative and enlightening ways of looking at still unsolved problems. The ideas are explained in a clear, straightforward manner with frequent examples and illustrations. Because they do not contain unnecessary background material they are short and to the point. They require careful reading, study, and consideration. In exchange, they contribute knowledge to help build an unparalleled understanding of all areas of market analysis and forecasting.

Unless you are gifted with remarkable natural insight, then trading successfully is the result of a great deal of work. For most of those who can boast a history of profits, there were countless days and long hours studying the way markets react to various government reports, its changes in volatility, the speed at which it moves, its relationship to other markets, and periods of illiquidity during the day. From an unlimited variety of patterns, successful traders are able to find some profitable sequence that could be anticipated.

Perhaps the most important part of the "insight" achieved from this effort is the understanding of risk. For every position in the market, there is a risk. Although price volatility is often used to express risk, each trading style or systematic approach to the market has its own specific pattern of exposure. A long-term trend following system, that can hold a long position for months, has the potential for a much larger profit or loss on that one trade than a day-trading method which is in and out within six hours. The sequence of profits and losses, however, form a very different equity picture than individual trades. When you define the rules for buying and selling, you must also understand the adverse price moves that are an integral part of that trading method; you must study those risks and manage them. There is no longevity without risk control.

John Sweeney tactfully calls those large, distressing price moves that we have seen in the past, and expect to see again, the *maximum adverse excursion*. These equity drawdowns are the difference between expected and actual performance—if the actual is much larger than expected, you are not able to stay with your plan, no matter how sound the theory seems. In a very realistic and practical evaluation of equity swings, Mr. Sweeney shows how a simple and thorough assessment of adverse price moves can yield very specific rules for risk management and greatly improved results.

Every trading method has its own unique pattern of adverse moves. These patterns, when studied in a systematic way, will show the amount of capital needed to trade successfully, and even the specific stop-loss, or maximum risk, that should be taken for any one trade. Once you see how it is done for one series of trades, it is easy to apply to your own performance. Mr. Sweeney takes these patterns further and shows how betting methods, that is, changing the size of the investment after profits and losses, can be designed to alter the returns and risk of a trading program.

While the author cannot possibly cover all the different trading methods, he gives the readers the tools and the understanding to continue themselves. To help further, he has separated the development and teaching of the analytic methods, from the spreadsheet code and numerous clear examples in the Appendixes. In this way he has made the Appendixes into a useful workbook and an important review.

You will find that the true value of John Sweeney's effort is in the way he methodically organizes, displays, and evaluates the adverse equity moves, as well as the favorable, profitable ones. It is this straightforward, understandable approach that is most rewarding for a reader. As he proceeds through the steps, we can see the conclusions unfold. By the end of the book, you will be able to say that there is a great deal to be gained by careful review and assessment of the adverse equity swings of your own trading approach.

PERRY J. KAUFMAN

Wells River, Vermont

PREFACE

This is a book about losses, but don't let your eyes glaze over. Risk—loss—is tied up with your fear, your profitability, and your career. For the most part, this book is addressed to people with Investment Committees and Lines of Authority to deal with, people who end up explaining themselves if things go badly.

For those people, this book presents a novel approach to assessing the extent of risk and minimizing losses. In the world of futures, the game is approximately zero-sum: for every winner there's a loser. Stock traders have it easier because their pie is (currently) expanding and, in many situations, everyone can win (or all go down together). But, in a futures game (keep the word "game" in mind), things are tighter. If I win, you lose. If you figure in commissions and "slippage," we both come up shorter than we'd like.

From such a straightened trading environment, and from mathematical theory, we know going in to the competition that the key to winning is minimizing the size of our largest loss. The problem, as with all trading maxims, is: what's large? How can this be quantified? That's where this book becomes novel.

I suggest you look at the results of your trading approach, consistently applied, to quantify things. If your trader's eye is focused on the bark or the branches of the tree, you may have missed the forest's moving, or at least swaying in the breeze of the business cycle. Unless you've kept a detailed diary and read it, you've probably not noticed any particular consistency in the after-entry behavior of the market. Each situation appears specific. That's why you get paid the big bucks: to be on top of the situation and trade smart.

Here's a thought for you, though: Shouldn't there be a consistent pattern to what happens when you take action? What if, instead of gut feelings, you could know objectively when to cut off a loser? What if, instead of gut feelings, you could know when to put in a protective stop? What if you could know objectively when to take profits? Well, if all that were possible, all you would have to do is execute your scheme properly.

From a management point of view, what if there were a way of assessing whether your traders were smart or lucky? What if there were a way of consistently winning trading profits other than putting the best and the brightest traders on the firing line until they burned out? What if you could put up an objective performance benchmark, quantify the amount of capital a trader needed (for his style and approach), and assess the inevitable losses as normal or abnormal?

Now there is such a method, but it requires work: poking into market behavior and using tools that aren't easy to manipulate. This book looks at what happens when we make decisions on a consistent basis—what happens to our trading positions as a result of the market's behavior? It asks, "If we consistently do this, what does the market do?" (This is different from asking, "If we consistently do this, do we make a profit?") When this question is asked today, the answer is "I don't know" or "It's random" or, worse, "I know it's going to be a winner (since no one consciously takes losers)."

The answer closest to correct is "I don't know." Think about it: if your market's truly random, nobody should be trading. In fact, trading would be impossible because the next price would rarely be close to the previous price—it might be anywhere.

Day to day, some speculative trades win, some lose, some go nowhere. We're interested in the winners and we want to find and eliminate the losers as soon as possible so as to keep our losses small. Actually, if we know what we are doing, we'll find that winning and losing trades look different and the way they "look" can be the key to success.

You might ask "What do you mean . . . how does a trade look?" I use the word "look" specifically to mean "appear" because I'm going to show you pictures of that behavior, pictures that are graphs which are collections of data. You're going to "see" the market's behavior in descriptive statistical terms rather than in price charts.

On these charts, you're going to see a line, the elusive edge that trader's seek and it will be a line all your own, from which profits can flow with minimized, quantifiable risk.

Do the markets exhibit a consistent behavior? Can we possibly adduce a consistency in what we see and experience? If so, what might it be? Well, open your mind and read on.

It occurred to me as I prepared my manuscript, that this entire book is really an exercise in exploratory statistics for traders. All the things we're used to seeing—charts, lines, indicators—have been replaced with graphs and tables; alien displays we traders don't use much. The book is organized to show you the nuts and bolts of excursion analysis without delving into the theory.

I use examples, rather than generalities. I've used spreadsheets because most "computerized" traders have one available. There is more elaborate software available for exploratory data analysis, but you'd probably need a degree in statistics plus considerable facility in programming to use it. (See the program Matlab from The Mathworks, Inc., 24 Prime Park Way, Natick, MA 01760-1500. Phone 508-647-7000.)

Luckily, the data we're examining is sufficiently sparse and simple that bonehead stat works fine. Still, it would be a great benefit for you, if you're not numerically inclined, to pick up not only the technique of measuring excursion but also that of visualizing happenstance graphically. Within straightforward limitations that you'll see here, the data displays can be applied to many aspects of your trading experience.

JOHN SWEENEY

Seattle, Washington
October 1996

CONTENTS

MAXIMUM
ADVERSE
EXCURSION

1

THE IDEA

Imagine that you are a prehistoric hunter at an African waterhole. It's dusk, dusty but cooling, the wind out of the north so that the animals, thousands of them, are easing up from the south along a wide, gentle-sloped valley, seeking water. You and your mates are hidden in the bushes to the south as well, but to the sides of the zebras' advance.

You're hungry and so is everyone at home. Roots, insects, a few fruits, and berries aren't cutting it this late in the summer. You've got to hunt and hunt successfully.

Hunting, however, is tough. You're short of spears and arrows. In addition, somebody usually gets hurt mixing it up with the animals; you use a lot of scarce energy; sometimes you're being hunted while you're hunting; and half the time, you come up with nothing except exhaustion because you don't have a theory of zebras.

You don't know anything about zebra physiology, psychology, seasons or, for all you know thoughts, let alone their gods. You never know exactly what the animals are going to do. Spooked from the north, you've seen them wheel and go south along the valley or sweep in a broad arc southward up the sides of the valley and then down (once they even went over the crest!), or even stampede right over the top of the hunters.

Even so, you've got to hunt. You're betting today that if the zebras are spooked simultaneously from the west, northwest, northeast, and east, they'll go straight back down the valley. Next, if experience holds, they'll slow down after a few hundred yards if not pursued and their tight running herd will spread out, right about where the rest of your band has moved in and set up to spear a straggler from all sides.

Even if the hunt goes as planned, keeping the carcass out of the mouths of lions or hyenas and getting it back home will be tough work in the dark. Still, you must hunt.

As a trader, your situation is a lot like the hunter's. Whether you have a team or are solo, you could use a theory of the market. You've probably got some ideas about what the zebra herd (the market) is going to do. You know the season is dry and which way the wind is blowing. You know generally where the herd heads when they break, you know how far they like to run when they stampede, and you know they will spread out when their fright dies down.

You'd like to make some money out of what you know. Are there better ideas out there? Trading is an oral tradition, surprising in the amount of money risked on fairly light formal credentials. As you learn, you get lots of profundities ("Keep your losses small," "Don't overtrade," etc.), lots of people with ideas, and books like this one but a theory is something different.

In the scientific method, a theory is the result of observation which leads to a provisional hypothesis of cause and effect, a hypothesis susceptible to testing. Testing will, with proper design, lead to confirmation or rejection of the hypothesis. After confirmation, further hypothesizing and testing continues; after rejection, the hypothesis is reworked and retested. Finally, a theory can be formulated.

Only in relatively modern times have such processes been applied to market behavior,* that is, the behavior of groups in open, unre-

---

* For a look at markets in laboratories, see work by Vernon Smith and his colleagues at the Economic Science Laboratory for Research and Education, University of Arizona, McClelland Hall 116, Tucson, AZ, 85721. See also the new field of behavioral finance at web site http://www.sas.upenn.edu/~rrottgen/finpsy.html. At this writing, only bits and pieces of research have popped up to indicate anomalies in classical market theory. For example, beta's explanatory power for returns is

stricted markets. As a result, our knowledge of how markets will act or react is abysmal. We are in the first stage of the scientific method: simple observation.

EXPERIENCE

Traders pick up experience while observing the market, but true experience comes from trading. Some keep notes mentally, some keep a journal, some even keep a database.* A running discussion among traders, economists, analysts, and the entire world also goes on, the result of which is the trader's view: his outlook for the economy, his market and his tradeable. Ideally, people record their views, their trades, and their results. "Mistakes" and "successes" are recorded and, over time, something is learned. Realistically though this work of recording is rarely done. Instead, there is an accretion of experience in a trader's head and a steady winnowing of losing traders.

Ditch that, I say, for statistically recorded results. Define your trading rules objectively and see whether they yield results that can help you define your actions operationally in the future. In other words, does the market act, after your decision, consistently or not? Since no one wins every trade, this is tough to tell. Still, it turns out that, in at least one respect, a good set of trading rules generates a classic set of "responses" by the market just as spooking a zebra herd at a waterhole does: You can know from the market's behavior (like the herd's) roughly what's going to happen.

If the herd, instead of fleeing, runs right at you, your hopes are dashed and you scramble out of the way. Instead of pursuing, you are routed with, hopefully, the smallest possible injury. It's a question of judgment. While you're in the act of spooking the herd, you're exposed. At any instant, they can decide to flee or come at you. You're dancing on the trader's edge, trying to decide if you should continue advancing and yelling—or flee for your life.

---

questioned now, over reaction by market participants is acknowledged and researchers are starting to attribute returns to market cap and market size or share.

* Chande, Tushar, $ecure (Chande Research and Trading, Pittsburgh, 1995). This software tracks a trader's actions and provides not only a trading journal but a checklist of factors to enter in the journal.

So, too, with trading. The judgment comes in when you must continue the trade or get out. The market is moving around in front of you and, like the zebra herd, is much bigger than you are. You must judge when it's decided to move favorably away from your entry or right back over the top of it.

On the floor you can see the orders coming to the pit, hear the noise, see the players screaming. Off the floor, you have the tape, your own order flow, your phone, and the chart—information passed by the recorder or the exchange's reporting system. Either way, you're looking to see how close the herd is coming. That's what you're tracking and it turns out it's a good indicator: past a certain point, they are probably going to run over you; before that point, they are more likely to flee properly.

THE RULE

Generally, good trades don't go too far against you while bad ones do. Sometimes a winning trade could go strongly against you before turning right, but what generally happens? What's usually the case?

It turns out that if your trading rules are consistent and can distinguish between good and bad trades, then, over many experiences, you can measure how far good trades go bad and, usually, see at what point a trade is more likely to end badly than profitably. That is the point at which you stop and/or reverse.

In this book, we will measure the price excursion from the point of entry. Measuring things abstractly from the point of entry gets away from the old news in the charts: support and resistance, value points. It gives us a point of departure in a constantly changing sea. In speculative trading, we only have our entry point and our exit points, so this is a valid point of reference. We aren't trading off a customer's hedge and we don't see the order flow or the issue calendar or the inventory. All these points of value aren't relevant to the technical speculator anyway; he or she really only has his price—take it or leave it. Moreover, that's the point from which we're judged. We may as well focus on it.

In zebra terms, we're going to see how close the herd comes to us before they shear off and head the other way—or decide to keep coming.

We'll tweak this analysis with some fine points later in the book and the general subject of using the technique in campaigning is dealt with in *Campaign Trading!,* an earlier book, but here we'll make sure the nuts and bolts of determining the breaking point of a trade are covered completely.

THE DATA

One other basic point needs to be covered before we start. The data for this exercise was developed for *Campaign Trading!* in mid-1995. It includes Crude contracts from October 1983 through October 1994, about eleven years of trading. The details of choosing and assembling the data were covered there. This process is unique to futures trading and equity or debt investors with long-lived tradeables can ignore the issue of continuity.

To provide long continuous charts, the most active contract data each month was put together with those before and after it in a data series such that the interday price changes while jumping from one contract month to the next were consistent. This process created the actual price changes one would have experienced in rolling from one contract to the next, but the values you may see here and there for Crude probably won't be close to the actual values published. The results, shown in the charts in *Campaign Trading!,* are realistic chart relationships and accurate day-to-day price changes.

I use daily data in my trading. I haven't experimented with intraday data though I have used the concepts in this book with weekly data.

2

DEFINING MAX ADVERSE EXCURSION

Try to think of future prices from the vantage point of today's prices. Imagine you are standing at a point looking forward toward a shifting gray cloud of varying density, each miniscule dot representing a possible price occurrence. There are points of greater density and other areas of near brightness. Looking directly forward, the mass is generally darkest but the cloud of possibilities shifts constantly as new information and new emotions enter the market and its participants. There are areas of concentration and others of relative improbability.

We're interested in the edges of the cloud. If we translated the haze of possibilities into tomorrow's price bar, the edges would translate into the high and the low of the day, the points at which our stops or limit orders would be last hit. We want to see if the shifts of the haze are likely to hit our stops if we set them here or here or here.

The shifting—the movement of the price possibilities—is described statistically as a *change* from an expected value, an excursion *away from* the darkest mass in front of us toward the outer edges of likelihood.

We can't actually look into the future and know what the excursion will be on any given day. We can only estimate what it will be by looking at its behavior in the past. The difficulty in this is deciding when to measure the excursion. If you measure it every day from yesterday (or the day before, or two days back or *n* days back), regularity is hard to discern.* However, if you measure the excursion more specifically, from explicit points in time, you may find a pattern. You should measure excursion from the point of operational interest: your entry.

Further, your entry should be defined by your trading rules which include your rules for exiting the trade. Hopefully, this definition is as objective as possible. If it's not, you'll find little regularity in your results or in the techniques described in this book. The entire premise of measuring your experience from the point of entry depends on your having defined the rules specifying the entry point and exit point precisely, *in advance*.

That said, I haven't found any particular set of rules more compelling than any other and perhaps even random rules may have merit.

In the end, the excursion you're interested in is that from where you get into the market. That excursion hits your stops or limits. This book focuses on stops, but excursion from your entry could also give you information on other entries, re-entries, or exits. (See *Campaign Trading!* for more on this.) Your entry point is where you've taken a stand and it gives you a point from which your assessment of the possibilities is measured and a point from which you can measure. It's a foothold in constantly changing markets. The standard price chart (Figure 2–1) is transformed into the chart shown in Figure 2–2 which is straightforward and focused.

The most exciting result would be if prices showed consistent behavior from your points of entry, no matter where the entry occurred or whether you were short or long. If that were the case, your trading rules would have the apparent ability to discern the future. It would look like Figure 2–3.

In practice, some trades are winners and some are losers in proportions varying by the rules chosen. However, charts something like Figure 2–3 do pop up. Charts of winners generally look like Figure 2–3 while charts of losers generally look like Figure 2–4.

---

* It's not impossible though. See Clifford J. Sherry, *The Mathematics of Technical Analysis* (Probus, Chicago, 1992).

Figure 2–1 Standard Price Chart.

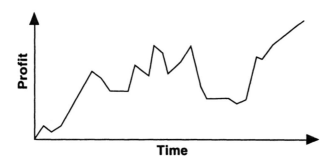

Figure 2–2 Raw Excursion. Starting from the point of entry, price excursion is measured as the gain or loss on the trade, not the price and exclusive of transactions costs.

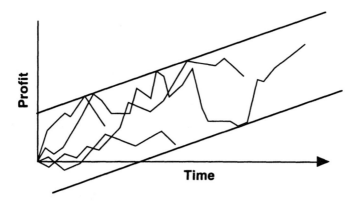

Figure 2–3 Consistent Excursions. The ideal result is a set of excursions from entry that behave consistently.

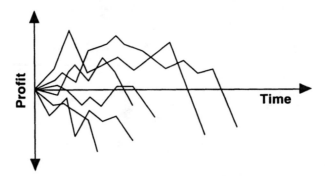

Figure 2–4   Losers. In comparison to the upward trend of the winners, losers for a given set of rules usually have a maximum upside, a shorter life span than winners, and a sharp terminating downfall.

Excursion, then, is just the change in price from our point of entry, measured every bar. It could be weekly, daily, hourly, or on the minute. Our interest is in whether there is some regularity in the excursion from entry, whether the position is long or short. If there is some pattern, some regularity, we hope to exploit it while we're in the trade by discerning whether things are going properly or badly and, in either case, what likely events are next.

ADVERSE EXCURSION, FAVORABLE EXCURSION

When prices move against your trade, that is *adversity*. From this comes the term *adverse excursion* which is used to describe that price movement which goes against our favor during a trade. The abbreviation used throughout the book is MAE—maximum adverse excursion—which is an acronym for the worst that it gets while in a particular position.

A key assumption for defining adverse or favorable price movement is the time frame. After all, if you wait long enough after an entry, just about any price might pop up. To avoid this, your trading rules must specify not only an entry, but also an exit. By doing this, you also define a time horizon in which you can analyze price movement.

Conversely, there is favorable price movement. Maximum favorable excursion (MaxFE) and minimum favorable excursion (MinFE) are discussed next.

MaxFE and MinFE

Adverse excursion is the greater of zero or the difference between your entry price and the worst price experienced after entry but before the trade is closed. If you're long:

$$\text{MAE}_{\text{Long}} = \text{MAX}[0, (\text{Entry price} - \text{Lowest subsequent low}),$$
$$\text{Previous value}]$$

MAX here refers to the greater of zero or the absolute value of the computed difference. If you're short, it's:

$$\text{MAE}_{\text{Short}} = \text{MAX}[0, (\text{Highest subsequent high} - \text{Entry price}),$$
$$\text{Previous value}]$$

Remember that zero is greater than a negative number. As for *maximum* favorable excursion, if you're long, it's:

$$\text{MaxFE}_{\text{Long}} = \text{MAX}[0, (\text{Highest subsequent high—Entry price}),$$
$$\text{Previous value}]$$

and, for shorts:

$$\text{MaxFE}_{\text{Short}} = \text{MAX}[0, (\text{Entry price} - \text{Lowest subsequent low}),$$
$$\text{Previous value}]$$

For *minimum* favorable excursion, if you're long, calculate:

$$\text{MinFE}_{\text{Long}} = \text{Max}[0, \text{Highest subsequent low} - \text{Entry price}),$$
$$\text{Previous value}]$$

and, if you're short, calculate:

$$\text{MinFE}_{\text{Short}} = \text{MAX}[0, (\text{Entry price} - \text{Lowest subsequent high}),$$
$$\text{Previous value}]$$

Examples of Maximum Adverse Excursion are shown in Figure 2–5. Maximum Favorable Excursion is illustrated in Figure 2–6 and Minimum Favorable Excursion is illustrated in Figure 2–7.

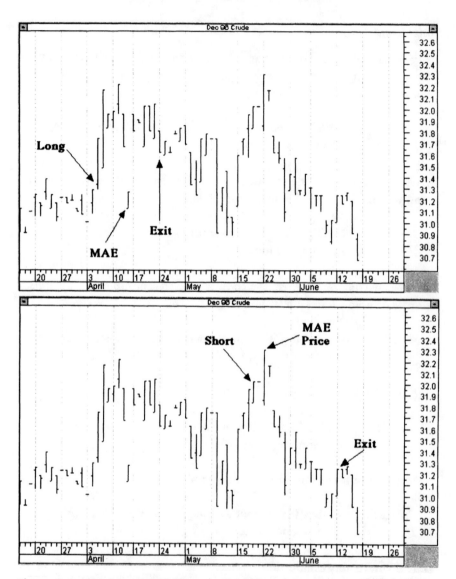

Figure 2–5   (Top) Long MAE Example. Price rises from the entry on the opening but just one day is far lower than the others between entry and exit. The low on that day will be used for calculating the adverse excursion on the trade.

(Bottom) Short MAE Example. A short comes early in this example and suffers through 35 points of adverse price movement before vindication. The absolute value of the difference between the entry price and the MAE price will be the MAE value for this trade.

Figure 2–6   (Top) Favorable Excursion When Long. Mid-July's price just tops early May's during this extended mid-1991 trade in NY Light Crude. The absolute value of the difference between the MaxFE price and the entry will be the MaxFE.

(Bottom) Short MaxFE Example. Another early short gets as far as $48 per share before rebounding into the $50s. The difference between the $52 entry price and the $48 low will be the Maximum Favorable Excursion of $4.

Figure 2–7 (Top) Long MinFE Example. As the NASDAQ composite rises steadily in early 1995, the Minimum Favorable Excursion rises along with it. MinFE often turns out to be a better indicator of a successful trade than MaxFE.

(Bottom) Short MinFE Example. As Westinghouse declines below $28 in early 1994, the Minimum Favorable Excursion price level from a short declines with it. The absolute difference between the entry price and the MinFE price never gets smaller.

I've never had too much trouble getting the idea of excursion across when explained with examples. Most people can see it as a simplified price chart connecting highs or lows from the point of entry. If there's a difficulty, it's in believing there could be any regularity in these graphs of excursion over time. That there could be consistency in how far they move from the point of entry also seems unlikely to people.

For some sets of entry/exit rules, there is no consistency. These rules don't have the ability to distinguish between good and bad trades. So, to that extent, people are right to be concerned. The only way to determine this is to look and see. If there is no regularity, then with your rules, you have little basis for trading. If there is, a potentially profitable strategy becomes possible.

In excursion analysis, we're concerned with the extremes of movement so we can analyze stop placement, limit entry, or optimal exit. All these occur at the extremes of price ranges. Moreover, without intraday data, we have no way of knowing what goes on inside price bars. The limitations of the typically available data force us to deal with what we do know—even so we should keep in mind that highs and lows are so thinly traded that the values reported can only be considered rough targets.

TWEAKING STOPS

A "tweak" is a small analytical adjustment which, while not central, may offer benefits.

In analyzing stops, we usually look for just one violation of a given price level, thinking that's where our stop will be triggered. You could require one, two, three, or more violations if you had intraday data. To satisfy this requirement, the levels at which these semi-stops might be triggered would be lower (for highs) or higher (for lows), allowing tighter "stops." Operationally, this would require being there to monitor action tick by tick, something most traders will not want to do, but it might be feasible for someone who's trading that way anyway and is sufficiently automated.

For those aware of differing speeds with which Treasury Bonds or some other tradeable move up and down, a further refinement would be to separate the data by longs and shorts. I once checked

Table 2–1 Calculating Long MAE. This position opened 7/11/94 on the close at 18.94. Since it was long (the negative 18.94 refers to a cash outflow), The MAE computations referred to the subsequent lows.

Date	Open	High	Low	Close	Long at 18.94	MAE Computation	MAE
7/12/94	19.15	19.28	18.93	19.09	−18.94	= MAX[0,(18.94 − 18.93),0]	0.01
7/13/94	19.08	19.26	18.81	18.96	−18.94	= MAX[0,(18.94 − 18.81),.01]	0.13
7/14/94	19.05	19.13	18.93	19.04	−18.94	= MAX[0,(18.94 − 18.93),.13]	0.13
7/15/94	19.00	19.01	18.85	18.85	−18.94	= MAX[0,(18.94 − 18.85),.13]	0.13
7/18/94	18.62	18.64	18.45	18.64	−18.94	= MAX[0,(18.94 − 18.45),.13]	0.49
7/19/94	18.48	18.75	18.43	18.75	−18.94	= MAX[0,(18.94 − 18.43),.49]	0.51
7/20/94	18.77	18.80	18.62	18.76	−18.94	= MAX[0,(18.94 − 18.62),.51]	0.51
7/21/94	18.66	18.93	18.64	18.87	−18.94	= MAX[0,(18.94 − 18.64),.51]	0.51
7/22/94	19.00	19.07	18.93	19.01	−18.94	= MAX[0,(18.94 − 18.93),.51]	0.51
7/25/94	18.89	18.95	18.78	18.85	−18.94	= MAX[0,(18.94 − 18.78),.51]	0.51
7/26/94	18.84	18.90	18.69	18.78	−18.94	= MAX[0,(18.94 − 18.69),.51]	0.51

Treasury Bonds in the late 1980s but found no noticeable difference in the MAEs.

SAMPLE CALCULATIONS

We're not dealing with involved mathematics here but to make sure the technique is clear, I'm including a tabular example as well. Many traders are very uncertain about mathematics but there is very little math to worry about with this technique. We're just comparing new highs/lows to (1) previous highs/lows, (2) previous maximum values,*

---

* The MAX function in a spreadsheet selects the highest value from the three values separated by a "," within the square brackets "[ ]."

Table 2-2 Calculating MAE When Short. This position opened 12/21/93 on the close at 15.12 (a positive value referring to a cash inflow from the short). The MAE computations referred to the subsequent highs.

Date	Open	High	Low	Close	Short at 15.12	Computation	MAE
12/27/93	15.32	15.32	14.86	14.90	15.12	= MAX[0,(15.32 − 15.12),0]	0.20
12/28/93	14.91	14.97	14.78	14.84	15.12	= MAX[0,(14.97 − 15.12),.2]	0.20
12/29/93	14.96	15.15	14.88	15.13	15.12	= MAX[0,(15.15 − 15.12),.2]	0.20
12/30/93	15.07	15.18	14.89	14.92	15.12	= MAX[0,(15.18 − 15.12),.2]	0.20
1/3/94	14.96	15.34	14.96	15.29	15.12	= MAX[0,(15.34 − 15.12),.2]	0.22
1/4/94	15.23	15.43	15.13	15.39	15.12	= MAX[0,(15.43 − 15.12),.22]	0.31
1/5/94	15.55	15.99	15.54	15.93	0.00	= MAX[0,(15.99 − 15.12),.31]	0.87

Table 2-3 Calculating MaxFE When Long. MaxFE grows steadily as a long position advances favorably. Longs compare the highest high to date with the entry price.

Date	Open	High	Low	Close	Long at 15.88	Computation	MaxFE
4/7/94	15.95	15.97	15.66	15.69	−15.88	= MAX[0, (15.97 − 15.88),0]	0.09
4/8/94	15.68	15.75	15.62	15.70	−15.88	= MAX[0, (15.97 − 15.88),.09]	0.09
4/11/94	15.70	16.05	15.68	15.96	−15.88	= MAX[0,(16.05 − 15.88),.09]	0.17
4/12/94	15.93	16.03	15.77	15.82	−15.88	= MAX[0, (16.05 − 15.88),.17]	0.17
4/13/94	15.86	15.96	15.76	15.90	−15.88	= MAX[0, (16.05 − 15.88),.17]	0.17
4/14/94	16.03	16.07	15.79	16.05	−15.88	= MAX[0, (16.07 − 15.88),.17]	0.19
4/15/94	15.92	16.40	15.85	16.36	−15.88	= MAX[0, (16.40 − 15.88),.19]	0.52
4/18/94	16.32	16.46	16.20	16.31	−15.88	= MAX[0, (16.46 − 15.88),.52]	0.58
4/19/94	16.15	16.23	16.04	16.04	−15.88	= MAX[0, (16.46 − 15.88),.58]	0.58
4/20/94	16.08	16.22	15.96	16.16	−15.88	= MAX[0, (16.46 − 15.88),.58]	0.58
4/21/94	16.10	16.37	16.04	16.36	−15.88	= MAX[0, (16.46 − 15.88),.58]	0.58

and (3) our entry point. A series of prices and the associated MAE for a long position is shown in Table 2–1.

Table 2–2 is an example of a computation of MAE when going short.

Calculating maximum favorable excursion is similar. Again, compare the subsequent highs and lows to the entry point and each other using the formulae above. Table 2–3 is an example for a long position, calculating MaxFE. Table 2–4 is an example for short MaxFE computation.

These extreme values—MAE, MaxFE, and MinFE—are not always positive. Sometimes, for example, there is no favorable excursion. In this case, the MAX function serves to limit the value to zero (Table 2–5).

Table 2–4 Calculating MaxFE When Short. A short goes well at first but then turns bad. This experience makes the point that MaxFE never gets smaller.

Date	Open	High	Low	Close	Short at 15.12	Computation	MaxFE
12/27/93	15.32	15.32	14.86	14.9	15.12	= MAX[0, (15.12 − 14.86),0]	0.26
12/28/93	14.91	14.97	14.78	14.84	15.12	= MAX[0, (15.12 − 14.78),.26]	0.34
12/29/93	14.96	15.15	14.88	15.13	15.12	= MAX[0, (15.12 − 14.78),.34]	0.34
12/30/93	15.07	15.18	14.89	14.92	15.12	= MAX[0, (15.12 − 14.78),.34]	0.34
1/3/94	14.96	15.34	14.96	15.29	15.12	= MAX[0, (15.12 − 14.78),.34]	0.34

Table 2–5 Minimum Extreme Value. Here a short at the close of 3/28/94 goes so far awry that there is never any MaxFE. Not only do MaxFE, MinFE and MAE never shrink, they never go below zero.

Date	Open	High	Low	Close	Shorter at 14.33	Computation	MaxFE
3/28/94				14.33	14.33	−	
3/29/94	14.41	14.58	14.33	14.58	14.33	= MAX[0,(14.33 − 14.33),0]	0.00
3/30/94	14.55	14.67	14.43	14.65	14.33	= MAX[0,(14.33 − 14.43),0]	0.00

Table 2-6 Calculating MinFE When Long. Going long at 15.88 takes a long time to bear fruit as MinFE takes eight days to rise above zero. For many trades, there is no minimum favorable excursion.

Date	Open	High	Low	Close	Long at 15.88	Computation	MinFE
4/7/94	15.95	15.97	15.66	15.69	−15.88	= MAX[0,(15.66 − 15.88),0]	0.00
4/8/94	15.68	15.75	15.62	15.7	−15.88	= MAX[0,(15.62 − 15.88),0]	0.00
4/11/94	15.7	16.05	15.68	15.96	−15.88	= MAX[0,(15.68 − 15.88),0]	0.00
4/12/94	15.93	16.03	15.77	15.82	−15.88	= MAX[0,(15.77 − 15.88),0]	0.00
4/13/94	15.86	15.96	15.76	15.9	−15.88	= MAX[0,(15.76 − 15.88),0]	0.00
4/14/94	16.03	16.07	15.79	16.05	−15.88	= MAX[0,(15.79 − 15.88),0]	0.00
4/15/94	15.92	16.4	15.85	16.36	−15.88	= MAX[0,(15.85 − 15.88),0]	0.00
4/18/94	16.32	16.46	16.2	16.31	−15.88	= MAX[0,(16.20 − 15.88),0]	0.32
4/19/94	16.15	16.23	16.04	16.04	−15.88	= MAX[0,(16.04 − 15.88),0]	0.32
4/20/94	16.08	16.22	15.96	16.16	−15.88	= MAX[0,(15.96 − 15.88),0]	0.32
4/21/94	16.1	16.37	16.04	16.36	−15.88	= MAX[0,(16.04 − 15.88),0]	0.32
4/22/94	16.47	16.76	16.33	16.74	−15.88	= MAX[0,(16.33 − 15.88),0]	0.45
4/25/94	16.62	16.91	16.55	16.87	−15.88	= MAX[0,(16.55 − 15.88),0]	0.67
4/26/94	16.81	16.89	16.53	16.59	−15.88	= MAX[0,(16.53 − 15.88),0]	0.67
4/28/94	16.48	16.58	16.37	16.4	−15.88	= MAX[0,(16.37 − 15.88),0]	0.67
4/29/94	16.38	16.65	16.25	16.63	−15.88	= MAX[0,(16.65 − 15.88),0]	0.67
5/2/94	16.64	16.97	16.64	16.83	−15.88	= MAX[0,(16.97 − 15.88),0]	0.76
5/3/94	16.76	16.8	16.57	16.64	−15.88	= MAX[0,(16.80 − 15.88),0]	0.76
5/4/94	16.68	16.88	16.55	16.57	−15.88	= MAX[0,(16.88 − 15.88),0]	0.76

Table 2-7 Calculating MinFE When Short. Short goes bad after initial surge! The MAX function serves to capture the initial favorable movement and retain it as the ending MinFE value.

Date	Open	High	Low	Close	Short at 15.12	Computation	MinFE
12/27/93	15.32	15.32	14.86	14.9	15.12	= MAX[0, (15.12 − 15.32), 0]	0.00
12/28/93	14.91	14.97	14.78	14.84	15.12	= MAX[0, (15.12 − 14.97), 0.00]	0.15
12/29/93	14.96	15.15	14.88	15.13	15.12	= MAX[0, (15.12 − 15.15),.15]	0.15
12/30/93	15.07	15.18	14.89	14.92	15.12	= MAX[0, (15.12 − 15.18),.15]	0.15
1/3/94	14.96	15.34	14.96	15.29	15.12	= MAX[0, (15.12 − 15.34),.15]	0.15
1/4/94	15.23	15.43	15.13	15.39	15.12	= MAX[0, (15.12 − 15.43),.15]	0.15

Minimum Favorable Excursion tracks the least favorable price excursion from our entry. It compares the lows to the entry if we are long or the entry to the highs if we are short (Table 2–6).

Table 2–7 is an example of a short position from 15.12 and the computation of minimum favorable excursion, MinFE.

These examples help to compute the MAE, MaxFE, or MinFE for any one trade. For exemplary Excel code, see Appendices A, B, and C, respectively.

3

DISPLAYING MAE

AGGREGATION

In Chapter 2, I showed how to measure MAE, MaxFE, and MinFE. I included some sample Excel code in the appendices and, for such a simple concept, it generated a lot of "spaghetti" code. This chapter deals with the next problem in using MAE: assembling the collected measurements and displaying them in a way that makes sense and contributes to concrete decisions on where to put stops.

Personally, I like to see "pictures." I can inspect tables of results but I'm more comfortable with a picture of the results than with a table of results. Consider what would be the best way to show the long list of MAE measurements.

As a rule of thumb, having thirty or more trades that are losers and thirty or more that are winners should provide enough data to have reasonable confidence in the results. The list might begin as shown in Table 3–1.

Just these few items represent a lot of information, but picking it out of several hundred lines is problematic. The models in Appendices A, B, and C have the structure to eventually show day-by-day (1) time in trade; (2) MAE, MaxFE, and MinFE; (3) trade profitability and

Table 3-1 Collecting MAE Data. For each trade, MAE is measured and recorded along with the net profit or loss from the trade. In this data, commission and slippage are omitted but the analyst can easily factor this into the profit/loss computation.

Date of Entry	Entry Price*	Date of Exit	Exit Price	Profit or Loss	MAE
6/23/83	−31.04	7/1/83	31.18	.14	.07
7/8/83	−31.2	8/16/83	31.96	.76	.01
9/9/83	30.96	9/14/83	−31.22	−.26	.46
9/22/83	−31.17	9/23/83	31.21	.04	0.00
9/28/83	30.69	10/17/83	−30.34	.35	0.00
10/26/83	29.98	11/4/83	−30.31	−.33	.34
11/9/83	30.09	12/21/83	−28.74	1.35	0.00
1/2/84	29.03	1/16/84	−29.6	−.57	.64
2/10/84	29.36	2/14/84	−29.24	.12	.03
2/15/84	−29.26	2/16/84	29.34	.08	0.00
2/24/84	−29.78	3/16/84	30.13	.45	.06
3/29/84	−30.62	4/12/84	30.5	−.12	.25
4/13/84	−30.49	4/16/84	30.47	−.02	.02

*A long is represented by a negative price—the cash outflow in taking a long position.

(4) account equity, all of which will be used later. For now, this is the question: Is there any difference between winners and losers, any difference we can use while we're in the trade?

To get at this, separate the results by winners and losers as shown:

Win	Winning MAE	Loss	Losing MAE
.14	.07	−.26	.46
.76	.01	−.33	.34
.04	.00	−.57	.64
.35	.00	−.12	.25
1.35	.00	−.02	.02
.12	.03		
.08	.00		
.45	.06		

Tweaking "Data Slicing"

An enterprising analyst will immediately think of separating the trades by longs and shorts or by duration of trade. I've done this on the few trading rule sets I use, to little advantage. Still it seems to me that this could be worthwhile.

Inspecting these numbers, notice that the winning trades have very small MAEs while the losers tend to have larger numbers. This is the seminal observation about MAE and it verifies the experience of centuries of trading. The anomalous characteristic of the list is that there are more winners than losers, something I've rarely found in trading systems. To display the information in these lists, turn to the graphics portion of your spreadsheet. Assemble the two columns like this:

Profit	MAE
0.14	0.07
0.76	0.01
0.04	0
0.35	0
1.35	0
0.12	0.03
0.08	0
0.45	0.06
−0.26	0.46
−0.33	0.34
−0.57	0.64
−0.12	0.25
−0.02	0.02

When selected and charted, they should resemble Figure 3–1.

Generally, a rough linear relationship between the size of the loss and the size of MAE should exist while the MAE for winners will be

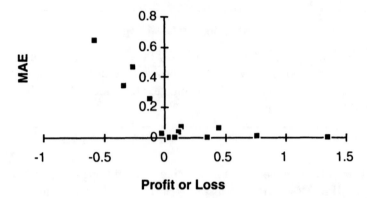

Figure 3–1   MAE vs. Profit/Loss. This analytical chart highlights the distinction between the MAE for winners and that for losers. The winners, to the right of the vertical axis along the horizontal axis, have MAEs less than .1 while the losers scattered to the left of the vertical axis, have MAEs greater than .1 (save one).

relatively small. If not, the market may have had a bout of disfunction or your rules may be unable to distinguish between winners and losers.

Stop and think for a second about how you're seeing trading data now. Instead of a summary table of wins and losses, Sharpe ratios, drawdowns, results for shorts and longs, and so forth, you're seeing a picture of your actual experience with, in this case, thirteen trades. You're also seeing all the market action from the viewpoint of the trade entry, not from arrows on a price chart. Isn't it striking that, from this viewpoint, there is some regularity to the market action? Seen this way, statistically, from your point of entry, might there be other "regularities?"

Putting up a chart like this serves to find outliers that may be real or artifacts. In our example, all appears normal: the size of the maximum adverse excursion rises as the size of the loss rises plus the maximum adverse excursion for winners stays relatively low no matter the size of the win.

Unfortunately, even winning trades can go bad a little bit. Looking at Figure 3–1, we see that winning trades might have a maximum adverse excursion of up to .1, which happens to be ten ticks. What if we knew for certain that any trade that went more than ten ticks bad would not be a winner? If it were not to be a winner, it would necessarily become a loser, right?

If we knew that, then, right in the middle of the trade, we'd have valuable new information about what to do. We'd see it go fifteen ticks in the wrong direction and we'd know we had a loser on our hands. Trading experience would tell us to get out while the loss was small.

Perhaps you're even more decisive. When the trade is put on, you put a stop at eleven ticks. You're ready to say, "Don't call me for a decision, just get out if it's to become a loser." You'd have automated the process of keeping your trading losses small.

Now, let's be realistic. We don't know *for certain* that a trade that goes eleven ticks wrong is definitely going to be a loser. From our sample of thirteen trades, we just have an estimate of that likelihood. I won't bore you with the mathematics of the statistical estimate. Instead, just look at the picture. You can see where the winners' MAEs cluster and how bad they get. From the picture, you can see how things go. Just keep in mind that unusual things happen in a market subject to countless random shocks. The picture enables you to estimate roughly where the good news stops and the bad news begins.

FREQUENCY DIAGRAMS

There is another type of picture of these numbers that gives even more detail and, later, will make better decisions possible. This type of picture is called a *frequency diagram*. If you are familiar with them, you may choose to skim (or skip) this section.

As the number of trades increases, diagrams like Figure 3–1 become a little rough for picking stop points and also for perceiving whether there is a distinction between MAEs for winners and losers. To get around this, categorize the data by the size of the MAE. (That is, by the size of the potential stop. We take the trouble to measure MAE so we can find a reasonable stop and/or reverse point consistent with our trading rules' experience.)

For a first cut, just make the categories equal to .1 or ten ticks. All the trades that have MAEs from 0 to .1, inclusive, will get lumped together. Then all those with MAEs greater than .1 and up to .2 will be lumped together. Then those greater than .2 and up to .3, and so forth. Now the data looks like:

	0 = MAE <=.1	.1 < MAE <=.2	.2 < MAE <=.3	.3 < MAE <=.4	.4 < MAE <=.5	.5 < MAE <=.6	.6 < MAE <=.7	.7 < MAE <=.8
Winners	8							
Losers	1	0	1	1	1		1	

The data are shown graphically in Figure 3–2. This kind of display is called a frequency diagram because it shows how often (that is, how frequently) trades fall into different specific categories which makes the distinction between the distributions of winners and losers quite plain.

Figure 3–2 is stark compared to the typical result with sixty or more trades but the distinction between the two sets of trades should be clear. You hope to find a sharp cutoff like this one for the winners but, if that's not possible, at least a distinct difference in the shapes of the distributions.

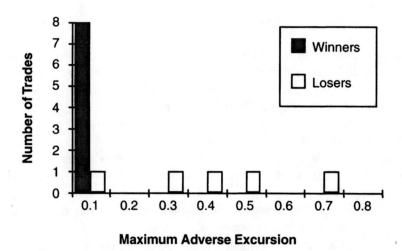

Figure 3–2 Trades vs. MAE. Converting the data to graphics highlights the distinction between the MAE distribution of winning trades and that of losing trades.

What you typically find is that the distribution of losers has a peak value somewhat to the right of the peak value of the winners. Another feature is that the distribution of losing MAEs has a long tail to the right; hopefully, but not always, the distribution of winners does not have a tail at all.

Ideally, the distribution of winners should have a huge cluster of trades in the very first category or "bin" with many fewer trades in the next few bins, then none at all in the bins to the right of the chart. It would look something like this Figure 3–3.

We're just fortunate that this sample distribution came out so neatly. The real world doesn't always work this way. For a taste of this, Figure 3–3 is the distribution from 3,069 days of trading data in a crude oil contract. (That's over twelve years.)

The two distributions are still clearly different. The distribution of losing MAEs goes far off to the right which indicates that many losing trades had adverse price movements. After many years of trading with a consistent set of rules, only three winning trades

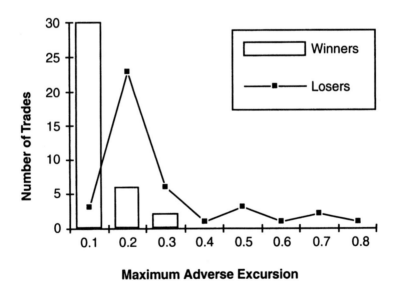

Figure 3–3 Trade Frequency vs. MAE. An idealized version of the two distributions shows the winners with a sharp peak to the left and the losers with a peak somewhat to the right and a long tail.

ever had adverse excursions of more than .45, a remarkable thought since .45 in crude is a loss of only $450 (The details of this trading system, a simple moving average system, are in *Campaign Trading!*)

Placing a Stop or Reversing

The point of all this effort is to look at something like Figure 3–4 and come to a trading decision, a decision that has nothing to do with entry or exit but only with controlling losses. You want to find a place to stop a trade that's going bad. The stop point shouldn't be too far away nor should it be too close to the entry point. Rather than look at retracements, wave counts, support/resistance levels, percentage price moves, arbitrary money management points, parabolics, or any of the other ways to pick "wrong" points, here you look at the experience displayed in Figure 3–4.

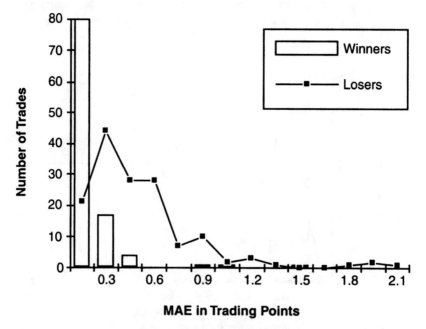

Figure 3–4 Exemplary MAE Distributions. The distinction after 252 trades is still clear. The distribution of winners does have a single trade each at .9, 1.05, and 1.5.

As a first cut (subject to a closer look in Chapter 4), you just eye-ball the graph and estimate where it's no longer worth your while to stay in. In Figure 3–4, points that suggest themselves are at .15, .30, and .45 away from the entry price. (These are the values on the horizontal axis.) Each represent a wider stop you could set.

Looking at Figure 3–5, the dropoff in number of wins as adverse excursion grows is striking. Hardly any winners have trades go against them more than .45, but there are three:

MAE	Winners	Losers
0.15	80	21
0.3	17	44
0.45	4	28
0.6	0	28
0.75	0	7
0.9	1	10
1.05	1	2
1.2	0	3
1.35	0	1
1.5	1	0
1.65	0	0
1.8	0	1
1.95	0	2
2.1	0	1
Totals	104	148

On the other hand, 55 losers go wrong by more than .45 from the entry point. Therefore, as a first cut, setting the stop at .46 would cut off 55 losers and convert three winners to losers. Setting the stop at .31 would cut off 83 losers and convert seven winners to losers. The most aggressive strategy would be setting the stop at only .16 where we'd have 80 winners and 172 losses. (You have all 148 losers plus you'd convert $17 + 4 + 1 + 1 + 1 = 24$ winners into losers for a total of 172.)

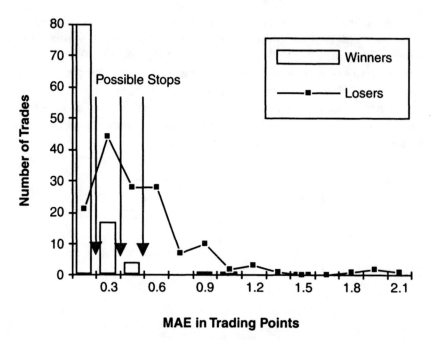

Figure 3–5 Possible Stops. Once an MAE diagram is drawn, it's used to pick points to place stops. In this particular situation, there seems to be little advantage to holding on past .45 where there are far more losing trades than winning trades.

There's clearly a tradeoff (which discussed in Chapter 4), but the cut at .45 is straightforward. It implies that to limit losses to, say, 2% of trading capital, you need:

$$\text{Capital needed} = (.45 \times 100) \times \$10/.02 = \$22,500$$

to trade this single risky strategy. (It doesn't mean that the whole $22,500 would be tied up supporting a single trade.) In this way, experience gives you a relatively precise estimate of your capital requirements and your stop-loss point, items that have been vague or without estimate in the past.

If those three winners are stopped out and converted to losers, what would that have cost? Would it have been better to stop out at .3?

This subject is covered in Chapter 4. For now, there are some details of this technique to clean up.

Picking Bin Size

For one thing, why should the categories we use be .15 or .30 or any particular number? Computationally, there's little to recommend any specific choice because today's spreadsheets can generate frequency diagrams very conveniently. The details of calculating them and generating the charts in this chapter are discussed in Appendix D, "Generating a Frequency Distribution."

The factors that control your bin size relate to your loss control. The point of making MAE charts is to find a point at which profits will be maximized with stops or reversals. Therefore, you want to construct the categories to help you find that point most accurately.

As a beginning point, there is your trading capital. Only a certain portion of that should be risked on any one speculative position and that portion is generally quite small, about 2%. At this level, your risk of ruin is quite small so the question is: Can you trade at this level of loss? Is there a stop point that is less than 2% of your trading capital? As a first cut, then, the category size should be no greater than 2% of your trading capital. Otherwise, you won't be able to see on the graph a stop point of that size or less.

On the hopeful thought that the stop point might be less, even considerably less, than the 2% level you could make the bin size half that amount or even one quarter that amount.

On the right hand side of the X-axis of your MAE chart, there is the trade with the worst adverse excursion. If it's huge and you've selected a very small bin size, you'll end up with lots of empty bins between those on the far left and those on the far right of the graph. From an analytical standpoint, you can graph just those on the left side that interest you (those with small adverse excursions), but from the standpoint of a presentation, such a large gap diminishes the impact of the information in the bars to the left.

The practical limitation on this fine division is often the amount of data you have—the number of trades. For strategies that don't trade often, you may have trouble coming up with thirty winning examples and thirty losing examples, let alone dividing the thirty into ten or twenty sparsely populated bins. There's no reason it should always work but my rule of thumb using a bin size of 1% of trading capital (that is, half the 2% loss limit) usually generates a workable display. If it turns out poorly, just change the bin values in your spreadsheet and recalculate.

Long or Short

It will have struck stock traders that I haven't distinguished between short and long trades and they have a point. Trading futures, I have rarely seen much difference between behavior in up and down markets with the exception of the bond market where the mathematics of yield makes a slight difference in the speed at which the market moves. Stocks seem to have a complete variety of price movement in both directions but I'm less familiar with them.

A trader suspecting a difference between the behavior of a short position in a stock and that of a long can keep separate records. In Appendix E, "MAE for Shorts and Longs," I've shown exemplary coding for tracking the MAE for shorts and longs along with an example of generating the frequency distributions used for graphs. Once you've generated the graphs for shorts and longs, you just make a judgment on the stop point for each and compare the two judgments. Whether they are significantly different or not is, naturally, yet another judgment.

4

DEFINING PROFIT BY BIN

PROFIT TRADEOFFS

It's all very well to see the numbers of trades that occurred in a given bin but, at some point, you'll want to know what the impact on profitability is as you widen or narrow stops. This usually comes up when you're trying to pick a stop point and you want to know if there's much of a profit difference between one level and another.

Perhaps two adjacent bins have nearly the same frequency of wins and losses—you're curious if there's much difference in profit when you set the stop at one bin's level or the other's, though you wouldn't expect it. More often, the frequency curve for winners slopes down nicely as that for losers rises. At what stop point do the "profit curves" cross? Were there one or two inordinately sized wins or losses distorting the curves? In other words, is the experience in your data reliable and should you make trading rules using it? These are all good questions, but let's define *profit curves* first.

PROFIT CURVES

In Chapter 3, I showed how to construct frequency diagrams or curves. "Curves" refers to the smoothed shape of the line between the plotted points.

Now, instead of plotting "number of trades," you want to compute the profit or loss on each trade within each category (or "bin") and plot the sum of those profits and losses for each bin. This seems straightforward, but there are some nuances to discuss after I've shown the process.

To begin, you'll have recorded for each trade its net profit or loss, including commissions. Comparing these figures to MAEs and your bin sizes, separate the trades into appropriate bins and total the profits.* For example, this table of trades:

Profit/Loss	MAE
−0.16	0.18
0.03	0.11
−0.55	0.55
0.16	0.00
0.07	0.03
−0.05	0.22
−0.21	0.21
−0.28	0.36
−0.16	0.22
−0.13	0.23
0.5	0.00
−0.06	0.13
0.02	0.25

---

* I use profits in the general sense here. Losses are negative profits.

becomes this:

Winners	
Bin	**Profit/Loss**
0.0 − .1	= 0.16 + 0.07 + 0.5
.11 − .2	= 0.03
.21 − .3	= 0.02
.31 − .4	
.41 − .5	
.51 − .6	

Losers	
Bin	**Profit/Loss**
0.0 − .1	
.11 − .2	= −0.16 − 0.06
.21 − .3	= −0.05 − 0.21 − 0.16 − 0.13
.31 − .4	= −0.28
.41 − .5	
.51 − .6	= −0.55

which computes as:

Winners	
Bin	**Profit/Loss**
0.0 − .1	0.73
.11 − .2	0.03
.21 − .3	0.02
.31 − .4	
.41 − .5	
.51 − .6	

Losers	
Bin	**Profit/Loss**
0.0 − .1	
.11 − .2	−0.22
.21 − .3	−0.55
.31 − .4	−0.28
.41 − .5	
.51 − .6	−0.55

Losers again show far larger MAEs than winners. To compute profit curves, segregate the trades by winners and losers, just as MAE trades are, and further categorize them into bins defined by the size of the adverse excursion.

This, in turn, displays graphically as shown in Figure 4–1.

Seen in this fashion, the tradeoff between setting stop/reversals at .21 or .31 is clearer. If this were all the trades available as evidence, you'd see there's little to be gained from putting stops as these higher values. (This is actually the last few trades in an eleven-year sequence of trades.) The losses taken at that level, both in number and size, outweigh the few wins kept by allowing the wider stops. You'd want a stop at .11 and no doubt about it. To make this point clearer when dealing with more trades than this, I usually plot both winners and losers profits/losses as absolute values (Figure 4–2). A summary display may be even better for some people. Figure 4–3 sums the losses and wins in each bin to give a single curve.

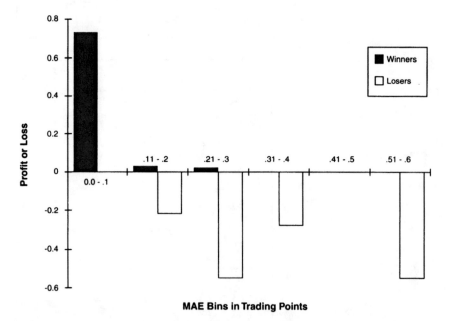

Figure 4–1 Exemplary Profit Curve. Shown graphically, the losers' losses vs. MAE are even more distinct. To aid in picking stops and reversal points, the losses' absolute values (the positive value) are usually plotted as in Figure 4–2.

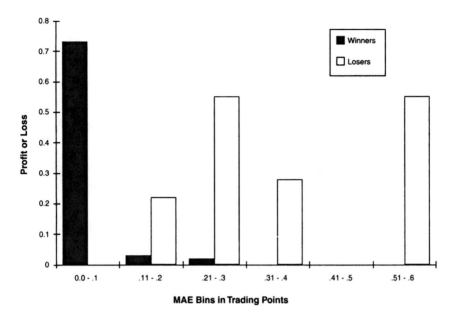

Figure 4–2 Absolute Value Profit Curves. To easily compare the size of the wins by bin with the size of the losses by bins, it may be easier to plot the absolute value of the losses. The format chosen for this display should be one you find easiest to interpret, since your judgment will be on the line when start trading this information.

Excel code for calculating all this on an automated basis, using the data format for the previous appendices, is in Appendix F. It's important to do this on an automated basis because too many errors creep in when doing it manually. Especially when you get enough trades to be statistically significant, you're handling a lot of data and the manual workload becomes burdensome.

Appendix F also shows how to generate three-dimensional charts that, in complex situations, may be helpful in picking stop/ reverse points.

INTERPRETATION

Normally, sample data won't be as clean as that shown here. The curves for the winners will probably overlap that for the losers far

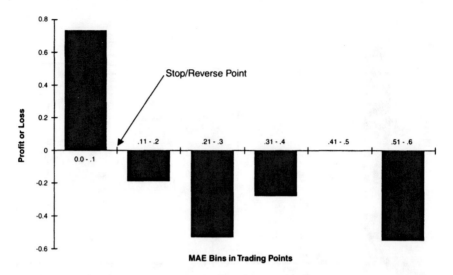

Figure 4-3 Total Profits. Summing the gains or losses from both winners and losers by bin clearly shows the point at which adverse price movement suggests a change in stance. Not only would stopping out at .21 be healthy, but there may be gains from reversing.

more than they did in this exposition. When this happens, you will make a judgment based on the overall trend of each curve and by visual estimation of the optimal crossing. Given the roughness of the numbers, your visual judgment is wholly proper and probably superior to mathematical algorithms.

Keep in mind that for these numbers to really work out you need enough occurrences to generate reliable estimates. If there's a significant difference between the frequency curves of the trades and the profit curves of the trades, the usual reason is that the number of trades falls off rapidly for the winners as stops are widened, thereby making the few remaining trades a greater influence.

Said differently, profit curves are very sensitive to the size of individual wins or losses. This is their limitation since one big win on a trade with a large MAE can make your curve look like Pike's Peak in the middle of the prairie. You need enough trades to make sense in the low MAE ranges and you should take the profits shown in the large MAE bins with a grain of salt. Typically, in the large MAE bins, you are looking at the results with virtually no impact from stops.

Sometimes, widening or tightening stops produces profit curves that seem very counterintuitive. Generally, as you widen stops, (1) winners that had been stopped out at a loss before become winners again, (2) losers that had been stopped out as a lesser loss become bigger losses or are stopped out at a more expensive loss. The net effect is dependent both on the frequency of each type of trade and the size of the losses they experience.

As you tighten stops, opposite effects occur. More winners are stopped out instead of going on to become winners and more losers are stopped out earlier to become smaller losers. In both situations, the effects are countervailing and we find the net impact by inspecting profit graphs. Whenever resulting graphs seem odd, inspect the tabular data for the trades that produced counterintuitive effects. You'll soon become familiar with these effects and be able to factor them in to your judgment about stop placement.

Whatever your judgment, you are certainly better informed using these procedures than if you were setting stops by arbitrary money management rules that bear no relation to actual experience.

5

IMPACT OF
VOLATILITY CHANGES

TWEAKS

With the basic concept of adverse excursion described in both text and example, turn now to slight adjustments in the concepts that might provide better results and, in any event, satisfy curiosity. In my days as an analyst, we always called these adjustments "tweaks" to indicate that, while they were not critical to success, they did slightly shift the odds in the proper directions. The next chapters are devoted to tweaking the use of adverse excursion in trading.

The first tweak relates to range volatility (as distinct from classical volatility). Then there's the effect of runs on the use MAE stops. Last, I take up issues of betting strategies.

Range or Volatility to Change Our Stops?

In focusing on price excursion, price *ranges* are the main concern. Highs and lows, being extremes, tend to be very lightly traded compared to the central values of the trading day. Nevertheless, if they do touch one's stop, your carefully placed order will be set off. The question for this chapter is to what extent volatility affects range which might, in turn, affect the adverse excursion measurements and the stop or reverse points that MAE suggests.

The intuitive idea is that, as intraday trading becomes more volatile than previously, ranges are likely to expand and stops become more likely to be hit, particularly closely set stops like MAE stops. Contrarily, if intraday volatility is lethargic, ranges will contract and stops are less likely to be hit (Figure 5–1).

Range and Volatility

There are many logical questions about this concept. First, do price ranges expand or contract with classically defined volatility? On this point there is some quick evidence. Experiences such as that in Figure 5–2 suggest that range is related to classically defined volatility, though not rigorously. Figure 5–2 is a mean-adjusted comparison of 20-day volatility with the 20-day average range. The qualifier *mean-adjusted* tells you that the means of the two distributions have been

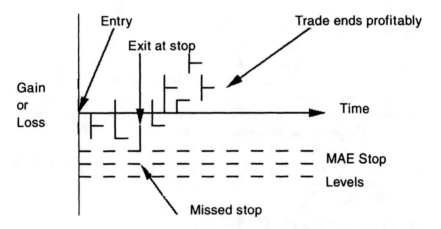

Figure 5–1 Adjusting MAE Stops. Stops might be adjusted as range volatility changes during trading. The hope would be that trades that would otherwise be profitable would not hit any expanded stops. Another possible benefit: Stops could be set more snugly during periods of low range volatility.

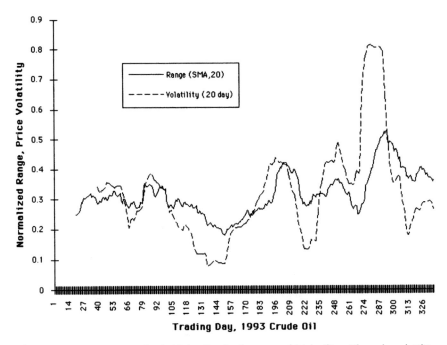

Figure 5–2 1995 New York Light Crude Range and Volatility. Though volatility fluctuates to relatively greater extremes than daily range, the relationship is often quite direct. In crude, range may be an effective proxy for volatility.

set at the same value by multiplying one series by an arbitrary adjustment factor. The result is a display that facilitates comparisons of the changes in the two series, not an analytical construct useful for establishing definitive relationships.

Figure 5–2 doesn't show overlapping lines but it does show changes in each series happening in roughly the same direction in reasonably comparable time periods. This is just one instance. Figure 5–3 is another example where changes in volatility and range might show some relationship to each other. You would need to run something similar for the tradables you use to get a first cut at whether this was a relationship you could use. It might be quite a study and this isn't the place for a detailed treatise on the relationship of range to classically defined volatility. I haven't found treatments of this subject in the academic literature, but it has been a subject of proprietary

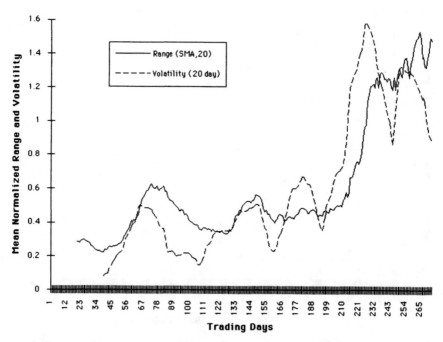

Figure 5–3   1990 New York Light Crude Range and Volatility. I picked 1990, a year of spectacular price fluctuation in crude, as an example of range and volatility coincidence.

investigation by traders and options dealers.* Anecdotal evidence in the form of charts in Appendix G suggest that range is a proxy worth investigating.

However, after looking at charts like Figures 5–2 and 5–3, I concluded that range might expand with volatility, but not necessarily or coincidentally. Therefore, to adjust stops for changes in price volatility was problematic; range itself would be the more direct indicator. The charts provided evidence that range did expand and contract *materially,* usually in concert with price volatility. Given that, the impact of range fluctuation was worth further study.

---

* Authors who have linked range and volatility include Cynthia Kase S&C Vol 11:10 (pp. 432–436); Andrew Sterge S&C V 7:12 (pp. 438–441).

At the Point of Entry. The second question about range volatility is whether, at the point of entry, you'll even know of a change in range volatility (or price volatility, for that matter). That is, will you know that it has changed or is about to change and that, therefore, you'll need to adjust the stop point right at the moment of putting on the position. Trading rules that enter upon breakout from a trading range or at the beginning of a trend will often come from a period of relatively quiet price fluctuation (Figure 5–4). The trading rule sees the sudden movement up or down, but the 20-day average range or volatility doesn't see the change as quickly due to the averaging process typically used.

It was this inability to "look ahead" that stimulated the development of MAE. Instead of trying to look ahead, MAE analysis asks "What is the actual experience of adverse price movement given these trading rules?" and "Given that experience, is there an operational difference that can be used at the point of entry?"

Taking that tack, you, the analyst and trader, need to examine what happens to range *after you enter,* using your trading rules. Just

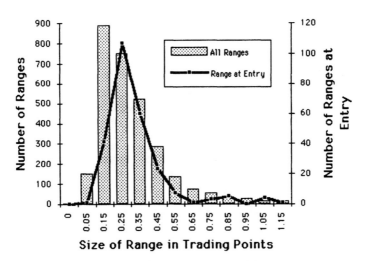

Figure 5–4 Range at Entry vs. All Ranges. The averages of these two distributions are identical: .32, but the distribution of all ranges is more peaked and skewed. Looking at this trend trading in crude, it's striking that entry was rarely from the most frequent ranges, the low ones at .15, but from ranges around .25.

as in MAE analysis, you may find nothing you can exploit. Your combination of tradable and trading rule may not identify periods of change in range. If it does give reliable estimates of changes in range, then you have the first prerequisite for adjusting your stops and reverse points.

For example, beginning on your point of entry just measure the amount the daily range exceeds the 20-day average range on the entry day. Another comparison that would smooth the data would be to compare the range each day to the moving 20-day average range. An example or spreadsheet of doing these is given in Appendix H and graphed data from both exercises is summarized next.

Comparing to the Moving 20-Day Average

Though this varies with the tradable, in my experience, if you compare the daily ranges after entry to the moving 20-day average *during the trade*, crude's result is common: the range doesn't vary statistically after entry. The daily range after entry, for the set of rules used here, is usually close to the moving average of the range. It's important to inspect your results visually as well as statistically, though.

Looking at Figure 5–5, you'll see plotted the range *after* entry less the moving 20-day average of range. The average value of this distribution is zero, but simply by looking at it, you can see that it's skewed upward and it's the skewed values that might hit our stops. In Figure 5–5, only one value goes below −.2 and that barely. In other words, range rarely shrinks more than 20 ticks below the moving 20-day average range. On the other hand, range often expands but it expands *episodically*.

Figure 5–5 shows only the occurrence that ranges expand by more than +.2. It's difficult to see when that occurs in the life of the trade. Transforming Figure 5–5 to Figure 5–6 shows that there is typically only one, occasionally two, days when the range expands by more than +.2. That is, to emphasize, range doesn't usually expand after entry and stay expanded. (This is specific to the trading vehicle and the trading rules. Your specific situation may give different results.) There is an occasional blip upward but it is not held. It is that blip that hits stops. (The shrinkage minimum of −.2 shouldn't be taken as absolute. Later, more data will show that it can range as large as −.6.)

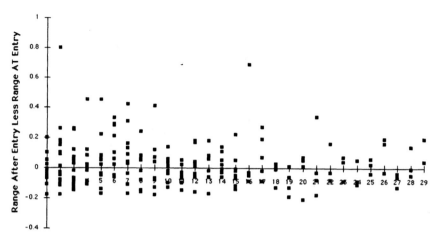

Figure 5–5 Range after Entry. Subtracting the 20-day range from the range on each day after entry often produces a plot like this. Most values for range are between −.2 and +.2 of the value on the day of entry. Also, while range rarely shrinks more than −.2 (range is limited to zero), it often expands more than +.2.

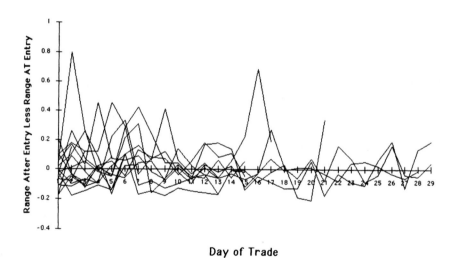

Figure 5–6 Range Expansion. Most trades don't show expanded range after entry on a consistent basis. By plotting range less range at entry, you can see that if range is to expand more than .2, it will do so episodically.

What about the difference between winners and losers? Is there any appreciable difference in the behavior of ranges? As with MAE, separate the two range excursions and plot to get something on the order of Figure 5–7.

Keep in mind that Figure 5–7 plots range after entry less the moving 20-day average of range; it's a difference not the actual range. Most of the values are less than .2 and most of them are around or slightly above zero. The episodic nature of the range expansion is there again: only one trade sustained a range expansion greater than .2 for more than one day. (That trade was the one winner whose range expansion was greater than .2 for five days.)

The average value of all the range expansions is slightly different. For losers, it's .00808, not significantly different than zero. For winners, it's .02602, which might be barely significant depending on your chosen level. (Keeping in mind that the measurements only go out to two digits, this citation is an example of statistical humor.) Parametric statistics don't capture the trading situation is displayed as illustrated in Figure 5–8.

In Figure 5–7, the mean is highlighted at zero with some skew toward the upside as suggested by Figure 5–6. The actual stats in Table 5–1, though, are not exceptional given the episodic nature of the range expansions.

Fortunately, for this set of data, if expansion is to occur, it will generally occur with winners. Add to that our knowledge from MAE work that winners don't generally move very far *against* the entry. Though this isn't always the case, the directional bias of winners is favorable (naturally!), so the bias of the range expansion we see in winners is generally (not always) favorable. Were it unfavorable, we'd see a greater amount of adverse movement.

Once again, your data might show different behavior.

Comparing to the 20-Day Average Range on the Date of Entry

Range at Entry vs. Range after Entry.   There's another way to look at it. The data in Table 5–1 compare the ranges *after* trade entry to the 20-day simple moving average of the range *during* the trade. The virtue of this is smoothing, but the future average range isn't a value you know going into the trade. You do know the value of the average range

Winning Trades

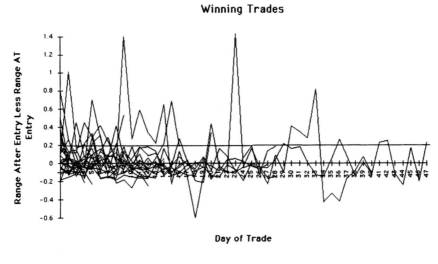

Losing Trades

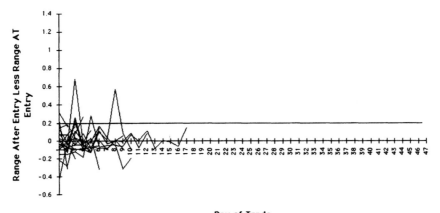

Figure 5–7 (Top) Winners' Range Expansion. With more examples, range can contract dramatically (one instance went to −.6) but rarely. More common is expansion going above the .2 level seen in Figure 5–6.

(Bottom) Losers' Range Expansion. Not only do losers last just a short time, but their range expansion is less than that of winners. Range contraction also appears more common in this limited sample.

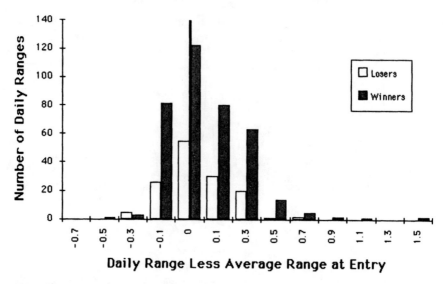

Daily Range Less Average Range at Entry

Figure 5–8 Range Expansion vs. Moving 20-Day Average of Range Winners' and Losers' Range Expansion Both Average Nearly Zero. Though there's a slight tendency to grow in both distributions, skew is just 1.1 for losers and 2.5 for winners. The greater frequency of winning examples stems from the fact that winning trades last longer than losing trades. (Note the scale shift on the X-axis.)

Table 5–1 Range Expansion for Winning and Losing Trades. The distributions described here are those in Figure 5–7.

n (Number of Days in Trades)	Losers 139	Winners 374
Max	0.68	1.43
Min	−0.43	−0.60
Average	−0.02	0.03
Std. Deviation	0.15	0.21
Skew	1.03	2.54
Kurtosis	4.27	12.48

on the day of entry. The summary of an analysis done in Appendix H compares (by subtraction) ranges after entry to the 20-day simple moving average of the range *on the day of entry* (Table 5–2).

Just looking at the statistical summary in Table 5–2, virtually the same raw data for Table 5–1 produce a different picture. Losers contract range about the same amount and winners more than double their range expansion from .03 to .08. The maximums for winners rise as well while the minimums for winners decline. The normalized statistics, standard deviation, skew and kurtosis, don't change significantly. The scale of the expansion? It's about .08/.32 = 25% of the 20-day average on the day of entry for this sample.

What are the shapes of the distributions of range expansions for winners and losers in this case? They are shown in Figure 5–9 and it's clear that the distributions are different. While the distribution for losers peaks in the −0.1 range (that is, expansions between −0.1 and −0.2999), that for winners peaks in the range between 0 and −.099999, experiencing some range contraction too. Despite this, the distribution for winning trades shows a very long, substantial tail to the right as well which pulls the mean over to .08.

It's clear that, in this sample—a sampling you'd do on your own tradable/trading rules combination—losers don't become losers because they drastically expand their range; instead, their tendency is

Table 5–2 Range after Entry vs. 20-Day Average Range at Entry. Comparing this table to Table 5–1, the distinction between winners and losers is that winners expand range by 8 ticks (.08 trading points) while losers slightly contract their range. The very high standard deviation for both winners and losers stems from the broad tails of both distributions.

n (Number of Days in Trades)	Losers 139	Winners 374
Max	0.73	1.79
Min	−0.44	−0.39
Average	−0.03	0.08
Std. Deviation	0.16	0.25
Skew	0.97	2.58
Kurtosis	3.75	10.58

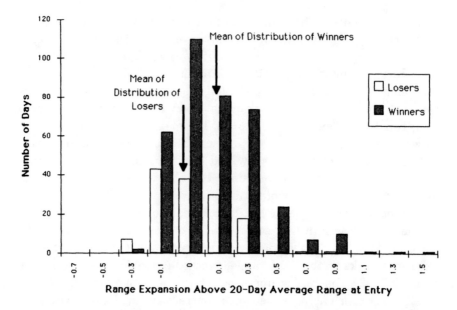

Figure 5–9 Range Expansion after Entry. In contrast to Figure 5–8, comparing range after entry to range at entry produces markedly different between winners and losers. On average, losers shrink their range −.03 and winners expand their range +.08. (Note the scale shift on the X-axis.)

to shrink their range, if anything. Winners, on the other hand, tend to expand their range after entry even though they have many instances of range contraction. Both distributions put almost exactly 50% of their occurrences between .1 and −.1, the means being pulled left or right by the tails. If their movement weren't favorable, this would place stops at some risk.

Are these two effects significant enough to affect MAE stops? To estimate this, compare the expansions to your MAE stop levels. For this data the MAE stops were generally .31 to .51. At these levels, the losers' average contraction of three ticks and expansions up to, say, 30 ticks would become contractions of 1 to 2 ticks and expansions of up to 15 ticks if the ranges expand or contract evenly (that is, on both ends of the range). These are well within the existing MAE stops.

Winners may be at some risk though. As it is, winners can experience occasional range expansions up to 90 ticks. If a winner's range

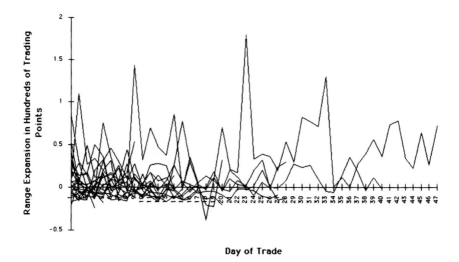

Day of Trade

Figure 5–10 Episodic Range Expansion in Winners. When measured from the range at the point of entry, winning trades in this sample had episodes of range expansion at many times during the trade. This figure compares to Figure 5–7 (Top).

actually contracts, there's no problem but what about the 50% of the times when it expands?* Does the winner's advance offset its range expansion? Recall, too, that range expansion is episodic. Do these episodes occur near entry when the stop is close or later in the trade? As to this second question, Figure 5–10, which plots range expansion by day-of-trade for the sample trades, shows that ranges of winners can expand at any time.

As to the first question, whether ranges expand faster than the advance of the trade, I've no evidence of this. Assuming ranges expand on both ends (the daily high and low) equally, an expansion of .04 (= .08/2) is not threatening to an MAE stop in the .3 to .5 range.[†] Comparing advances on a winning trade to episodes of range expansion during the trade will typically show the trade's profit growth

---

* Actually, in this sample, 53%.

[†] The data for your tradable and trading rules may not show the same result. This is just an exemplary analysis.

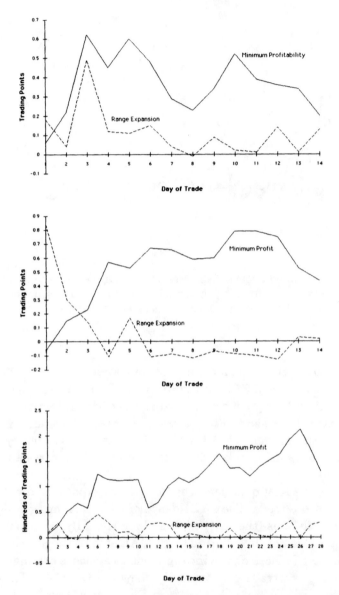

Figure 5–11   Range Expansion vs. Trade Advance. To see whether range expansion in winning trades is faster than the rate of the winner's advance, the two are plotted for inspection for several trades. "Minimum Profit" is, for longs, low minus entry and for shorts, it's entry—high. There was no evidence that range expansion outpaced trade advance generally.

outstripping any range expansion (Figure 5–11) but I know of no way of summarizing that experience.

Though your analysis might show stronger range expansion, the evidence in crude oil, for these trading rules, is that range expansion is a negligible influence. At most, you'd widen stops by half of the average range expansion or four ticks. This exemplary analysis and the worksheets in Appendix H would be the structure you'd apply to your own trading situation.

MAE versus Range at Entry

It's an intriguing idea: expanding the stops as volatility or range volatility grow in our tradable. It makes intuitive sense, but you need to check it out for your tradable. One way to do that is to compare maximum adverse excursion to the range at entry. If winners' adverse excursion is large compared to range, there will be grounds for expanding stops; otherwise, not.

For this example, I compared the 20-day average range on the day of entry to the maximum adverse excursion experienced during a trade for 252 trades in crude during 1983 to 1994. Thinking there might be a quantifiable relationship, I divided MAE (in trading points) into the 20-day average range (in trading points). The resulting distribution is in Figure 5–12 and shows, for this extensive data, distinct differences.

Part of this distinction is that already made: Winning trades don't go far against us, so their adverse excursion will be small and their ratio to range at entry will be smaller than that of losers. Does this difference tell us how much, if any, to expand our stops as range grows? Since losers will hit the MAE stop anyway, let's look at the distribution for winners

Looking at Figure 5–13, we can see that MAE is heavily concentrated in the ratios below 1.0. That is, MAE is generally much less than daily range. Average winners' MAE for this data was .11 while the average range was .32. Average *ratio* was .35. The ratios to the right of 1.0 on the horizontal axis amount to only seven instances. If, as a first approximation, half the daily range goes in the direction of an MAE stop, it would take a ratio of 2.0 (MAE twice as large as

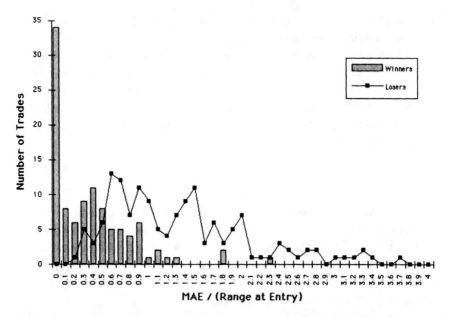

Figure 5–12 Comparing MAE and Range at Entry. Winners and losers show distinct differences in the relationship of the adverse excursion to the range at entry in this data from eleven years of crude trades.

range) to suggest expanding stops. Only one trade's MAE exceeded 2.0 though.

Throwing out the values of zero (for all the trades with no adverse excursion) and computing the mean ratio of the remaining trades, the average ratio turns out to be .52. In other words, the average adverse excursion during a winning trade that has *any* adverse excursion is about half the size of the range at entry, though there are episodes of much greater adverse excursion, as noted on the figure. Again, even this conservative basis doesn't suggest the need to expand stops.

No Problem?

The third question about the idea of expanding or contracting stops based on expanding range is whether the information we have already handles that. After all, the original MAE stops and reversals were

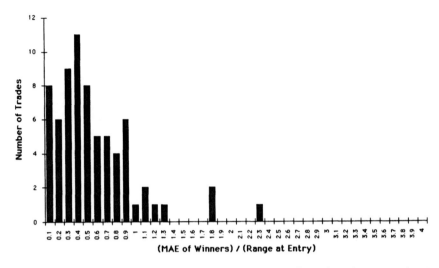

Figure 5–13 Winners MAE vs. Range at Entry. Recalling that the ratio of 1.0 places MAE and range at equality, winners in crude show barely enough adverse movement above 1.0 to justify any expansion of stops.

developed without checking for volatility. The values came from experience in *all* conditions of volatility. Therefore, the first assumption would be that the impact of volatility is already in the MAE distributions. Sharply distinguished distributions like Figure 5–14 show very few winners that would be cut off by stops set too tightly. On the other hand, distributions with extended tails of winners might be candidates for some adjustments (Figure 5–15).

Just taking Figure 5–15 as an example of the real world, expanding the stop from, say, .45 to 1.05 appears impractical. It would absorb far more losing trades than winners. Nor is the situation in Figure 5–15 unusual. Readers of *Campaign Trading!* will have seen many distributions where, just as the winning trades tail off, the number of losing trades picks up and this just as the adverse excursion is rising steadily, forcing the acceptance of larger losses as the stop is widened.

To boot, knowing as we now do (for crude) that range expansion is episodic, if we did observe extraordinary ranges before a trade entry

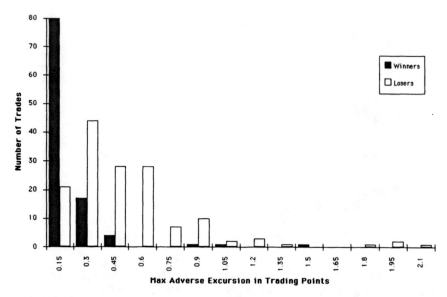

Figure 5–14 Different Distributions. Expanding an MAE stop from .3 to .45 because range volatility had heightened would expose profits to far more losing trades while possibly allowing only four more winners.

we might suspect that didn't mean much. One episode of widened range would not mean that more episodes were on the way.

Still, if it is possible to identify periods of extraordinary range volatility, would that have any impact on the stops to be used? Presumably, you'd know that daily ranges exceeded some "normal value" and positions taken during such a period would be equipped with wider stops. Possible sources for such volatility include news, seasonality, approaching expiration of a trading contract, or general surges in trading interest.

Normality. Most traders will have an idea of what a normal range is. Defining it objectively, though, is a little tricky so I'll step through a process that gives you an experiential idea of normal range. The "normal" range may turn out to be narrow and well-defined—in which case you would know if ranges you were seeing were exceptional—or it may turn out to be quite broad, too broad to effectively modify stop settings.

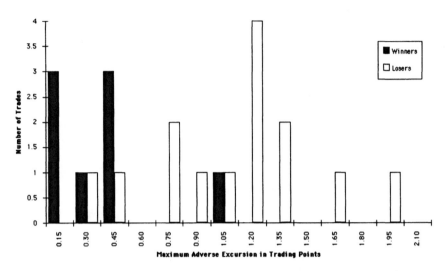

Figure 5–15 Mixed Distributions. In contrast to Figure 5–12, experience the sows winners with large adverse excursions may indicate a tradable whose range volatility could affect MAE stops.

For example, Figure 5–16 shows the distribution of daily average ranges for eleven years of crude trading. Since the range cannot go below zero, we end up with a distribution which is not normal as statisticians define normal. Indeed there were seven trading days with ranges beyond 200 ticks (2.0 on the chart), days I forbore charting. In a situation like this, what constitutes a "normal" range and what would constitute a range out of the ordinary?

Looking at the data in Figure 5–16 slightly differently, I've plotted the cumulative percentage distribution in Figure 5–17. Nonstatisticians should recall from math class that in a normal distribution, a mean plus one standard deviation will include 67% of all occurrences, all events. Add another standard deviation and you've got 95% of all occurrences—95% of occurrences being a rough idea of a normal range of experience. Figure 5–17 connects the range sizes along the bottom axis with the percent of all occurrences on the vertical axis so that we can ask what ranges are included in 95% of our experience with crude ranges.

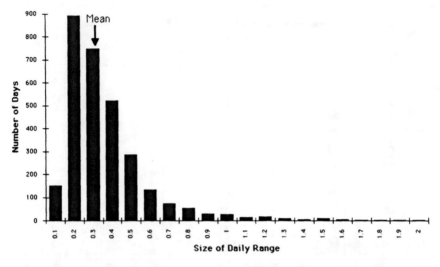

Figure 5–16 Distribution of Daily Ranges. From late 1983 until October, 1994, crude experienced the ranges shown here. The median for the distribution (.28) is not significantly different from the mean (.32) but there is necessarily a long tail to the upside that skews the perception of "normal" range.

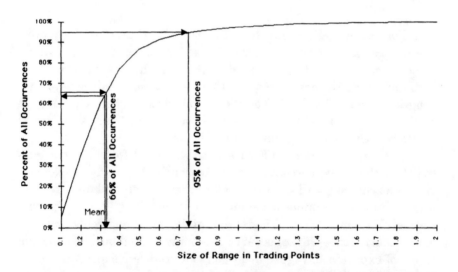

Figure 5–17 Cumulative Percentage Distribution of Ranges. The distribution of ranges for crude is concentrated so sharply that 64% of all occurrences are between zero and .32, the mean of the distribution.

Looking at Figure 5–17, the high concentration of ranges between 20 and 30 ticks causes nearly a full standard deviation's worth
of events (64%) to fall *at* or *below* the mean at .32. Recalling that
"normally" 67% or so of all occurrences will be within one standard
deviation of the mean (both above and below), it turns out that 67%
of all occurrences in this distribution fall between .01 and .34, just
two ticks above the mean range. That is to say, 67% of all ranges will
have a value between .01 and .34. This is good concentration but if
you wanted "normal" to include the more common standard of 95% of
events, you'd have to include days with ranges up to .75 or twice the
size of the average range. Where in this range do you start widening
stops? Well, if 95% is the normal range of experience, you'd consider
widening stops if you had seen daily ranges exceeding 75 ticks (.75
trading points). If, despite the logic above, you want wider stops, the
general rule is: widen stops when you're seeing daily ranges outside
95% of your past experience. How much you'd widen the stop would
depend on the range expansion you'd measured. In the crude data,
there were 13 average ranges above .75 with no discernible relationship either to MAE or size of win or loss.

Range at Entry	Profit or Loss	MAE
0.77	−0.32	0.32
1.07	0.87	1.38
0.87	−0.87	0.87
1.14	−1.64	1.92
1.10	0.77	0.90
1.07	−2.05	2.05
1.05	3.72	0.00
0.86	5.06	0.00
0.82	−0.70	1.14
0.88	0.48	0.00
0.83	−1.81	1.81
0.71	−1.27	1.67
0.74	0.15	0.13

SUMMARY

Expanding stops, particularly MAE stops, when range volatility rises is an intuitively appealing idea. Using excursion analysis, you can check whether it makes sense for your combination of tradable and trading rules.

Begin by summarizing your experience with the tradable's ranges using the cumulative distribution of ranges as in Figure 5–17. This will give you a sense of what the "normal" range is. Should you exceed that, go to step two.

Step two is to check the range expansion for both winners and losers. In the crude oil example in this chapter, it turned out that the range of losers actually contracted, almost imperceptibly while that of winners expanded. In any case of range expansion (Table 5–2), widen MAE stops by half the estimated range expansion.

In this example, I was surprised that crude oil showed range expansion up to 25% of its average range. My experience, certainly not exhaustive, is that range expansion is much more a perceived phenomenon than one that's measurable. Perhaps because range volatility and price volatility are episodic, human perception remembers most vividly the exceptional instances rather than the general rule.

6

RUNS EFFECTS

CAPITAL CONSERVATION

When using excursion analysis to develop information about adverse movement, one of the key benefits is getting a handle on how much money you need to trade the tradable/trading rule combination you're considering and whether you should trade it at all. Using adverse excursion information does three things:

1. Eliminates large losses. For the most part; huge gaps in pricing can still jump over your stops. Options users will have some protection even from this event.

2. Tells you how much capital you need to trade the combination. The combination of tradable, trading rules, and loss management you use.

3. Tells you where to put your stops on individual trades.

All of these things are crucial and, in retail trading, are often set by seat-of-the-pants guesstimates. Even commercial trading and money managers often have barely any defensible reasons for their loss-cutting tactics.

Using adverse excursion information, you can manage individual trades effectively and build up the ability to trade a variety of market modes, such as trending or ranging, and a variety of tactics, such as add-on trades, counter-trades, and reversals. The result is you are trading far more actively than you would at any one time in a single trading system.

Why is this important? What could happen is that, despite controlling individual losses, you could end up with a string of trades that impact your capital so severely as to stop your trading. When this happens, there is no chance of recovery and you've suffered the catastrophic loss that MAE analysis was designed to prevent in the first place.

In terms of trading management, a string of consecutive losses (a "run" of losses) has a direct impact on any individual trading tactic and on two management plans, the actual trading campaign itself and a subsidiary tactic which is not necessarily being used: a betting strategy.

IMPACT ON A PARTICULAR TRADING TACTIC

The most discernible impact of a run of losses is the drawdown in account equity while using one particular trading tactic. Since one tactic is all that most retail traders and many commercial traders use, their attention is quickly brought to any string of losses. This discouraging event causes many to abandon systematic trading rules that have tested well and turn out well again, despite the run of losses.

Experience is the best teacher for each tactic and most trading report summaries include an accumulation of *drawdown* (equity reduction, whether measured on an open-and-closed trades or closed-trades-only basis). It's impossible to say if traders using MAE are more likely or less likely to have trades hit by stops than traders using other means, so their susceptibility to runs is probably no different than others. MAE users can look at drawdown stats from standard software (using MAE stops) as a rough measure of their capital exposure. However, these "worst cases" aren't the best measure. You need to measure the drawdowns and inspect their distribution for information.

Having looked at those losses, you must decide if they are actionable and, if so, at what point. In other words, you cut off an individual trade's losses at 2% of trading capital but do you cut off runs losses? This depends somewhat on the frequency of runs generated by a trading combination. If your trading rules were such that you experienced lots of losses and only a few gains, the chances for a run of losers would be higher than a combination that produced mostly winners. Thus, to make the estimate, you must examine the record. The details of the example that follows are developed in Appendix I.

Frequency of Runs

The first thing is to define a drawdown and see if it exists as defined. By graphing account equity from a single trading tactic as in Figure 6–1 you can quickly see where prolonged periods of equity drawdown occurred. Figure 6–1 is the account equity from a single trading

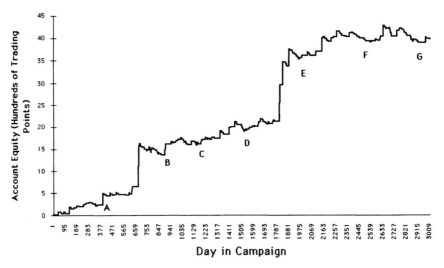

Figure 6–1 Account Equity from Trend Entry Tactic. Lots of small losses and a few huge wins typify trend trading. Here MAE stops have served to keep losses small but there are long series of losses to be endured.

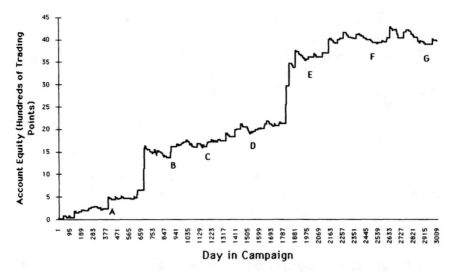

Figure 6–2 Equity Retracement Levels. Levels A through G are all retracement levels caused by runs of losses, what is usually called drawdown. Adverse runs' size is measured from the previous peak in equity.

tactic: entry on a dual moving average system using crude oil as the trading vehicle.* The stop used was .31 or 31 ticks, about $310, ignoring commissions. The result is typical for trending systems: a few incredible gains and lots of small losses. It's almost ideal for the study of adverse runs.

Looking at the periods of equity drawdown, most losses are roughly offset by small gains. However, in periods 700 to 900 as well as later periods around 2000, 2500, and 2900 there were "extended" periods of losses that slowly wore away account equity. You might pick out different periods that I should have included and that brings up the issue of definition. What's to be a run and what's to be a significant run against which we should guard?

Visually inspecting charts like Figures 6–2 and 6–3 repeatedly suggests one practical answer: An adverse run is any sequence of losses or gains (sic) resulting in equity falling below a previous peak and continuing until a *new high in equity* is attained. To measure an

---

* This system was described in detail in *Campaign Trading!*

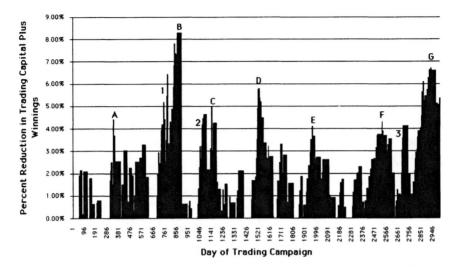

Figure 6–3 Drawdown Compared to Capital Plus Winnings. A run of losses builds drawdown up to 8% of initial trading capital plus winnings. Comparing equity reduction to capital plus winnings is only correct on a "one contract" or "no additional shares" basis. For a more conservative view, see Figure 6–4. Points A through G are those referenced in Figure 6–2.

adverse run, simply keep a tally of the previous peak equity and the current account equity, computing the percentage reduction on a daily basis. Plotting the result makes judgment of the level of significance and labeling the charts by inspection easier (Figure 6–3).

Figure 6–3 plots the percentage reduction from peak equity plus initial trading capital of the trading combination's various adverse runs. Pictured in this fashion, drawdown from adverse runs may show some consistency, consistency you could use to assess at what level to become concerned about a string of trading losses from a specific trading tactic. At a minimum, each peak in Figure 6–3 defines a drawdown in Figure 6–2.

In this figure, material peaks are those of 4% or greater equity reductions subsequent to new highs in equity. That is, a new high in equity ends the adverse run and that new high appears in this figure as a spot on the X-axis with no columns above it. Three peaks (1, 2, and 3) show drops below the 4% level before going on to their ultimate high but aren't noted because the drawdown had not yet ended. In other words, equity continued to decline after that interim peak was established, despite a temporary reduction in drawdown.

Figures like this make assessments of significance easier. However, if you want a completely objective standard, go with the original definition and count *all* the peaks interrupted by periods of higher profitability. Doing this highlights that, in a tractable trading combination, most of the drawdowns from adverse runs of trades will be fairly small.

Computation

The precise computation of "Percent Reduction in Trading Capital Plus Winnings" should be clear from Figure 6–3. Since we know the MAE stop ($310) and we know our 2% rule for the MAE stop, we can compute the trading capital required to support this trading combination. That is:

$$\$310/.02 = \$15,500$$

If you were trading two or more contracts or blocks of shares at the $310 stop, your available trading capital would be, for example:

$$2 \times \$310/.02 = \$31,000$$

It is to $15,500 plus any accumulated equity that Figure 6–3 compares the drawdown experienced by this trading combination:

$$(\text{Maximum equity} - \text{Today's equity})/(\$15,500 + \text{Maximum equity})$$

Figure 6–3 certainly shows some consistency. In eleven years of trading this combination, seven major drawdowns occurred. Though too few to be statistically significant, these occurrences may give a rough idea of the frequency of adverse runs. Size of runs is also roughly calculable: between 4% and 8% of capital plus winnings before going on to new highs in profitability. These adverse run effects should be bearable for most well capitalized traders but there is a caution: results are dependent on *when* the run occurred. Had the largest adverse run started on day one of the campaign, there'd be a peak of percentage reduction of:

$$(42.78 - 38.87)/15.5 = 25\%$$

instead of 6.5% at point G. This argues that, instead of comparing the adverse run to the trading tactic's equity plus the initial trading capital, it should be compared to the trading capital alone.

A More Conservative Standard

A winning trader has the luxury of banking the winnings and continuing to trade on the initial capital committed to the trading tactic. Alternatively, he can hold the winnings against future, probably inevitable, storms of adversity. Or, he can up his commitment to the particular tactic by increasing the shares or contracts traded, relying on his analyses of the MAE stop and runs to protect him. I advocate the third path. For those who pursue the first or second path, drawdowns should be compared to initial trading capital which is the subject of Figure 6–4.

Figure 6–4 shows more serious problems with adverse runs in this experience with crude. The 25% figure mentioned earlier is there to the right, but so are regular stabs at the 15% level. Larger adversities cannot be ruled out either. Indeed, in this worst case outlook, adversities amounting to 5% have more than a 50% chance of reaching 10% to 15%. Still, none of them amount to the 40% reduction in trading capital which is the most popular rule of thumb for suspending trading. If winnings are considered as well (Figure 6–3), none of the drawdowns remotely approaches 40%. That is, despite a very good likelihood of seeing an adverse run of 10% to 15% of initial trading capital, this combination's experience is that losses from such runs will be recovered and equity will move to new highs before seeing another adverse run of similar or greater magnitude.

Immediate Disaster

Finally, even eleven years' experience is only suggestive, not exhaustive of all possibilities. A single 40% reduction could happen right off

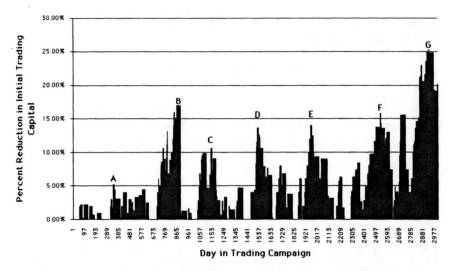

Figure 6–4   Drawdowns of Initial Trading Capital. A more arduous comparison than that of Figure 6–3 is to compare the drawdown from adverse runs of trades with initial trading capital, ignoring any winnings. On this basis, the experience with crude shows the possibility of 25% drawdown though most are in the 10% to 15% range.

the bat, putting you out of business. However, this small sample of experience suggests the possibility of a huge adverse run is small. There is no instance of 40% drawdown before returning to higher profitability. The probability of even being in one of the sample's 200-day drawdown states is about 45% and, once that hurdle is surmounted, the possibility of its being a 25% drawdown is one in seventeen. That works out to less than 3% chance at any one time for the worst case on day one. Actual probabilities may be even lower as shown next.

The likely extent of drawdown is suggested by the distribution of occurrences of drawdowns in the historical data as shown in Table 6–1 and Figure 6–5.

Looking at Figure 6–5, it's apparent that most drawdowns are small, even in relation to initial trading capital (vs. trading capital plus trading profits) and 70% are 10% or less. If you are looking at this kind of concentration, it's reassuring evidence that your trading combination is workable. That 94% of the time its drawdowns don't exceed 18% is also workable. Plus, it's worth keeping in mind that drawdown

Table 6-1 Frequency of Size of Drawdowns. From the sample data that produced Figures 6–1 to 6–3, this summary of every drawdown between periods of rising profitability was prepared. This sort of table gives you the relationship between the size of the drawdowns in your data and their probability, here summarized in Figure 6–5.

Trading Capital	Occurences	Probability	Cumulative Probability
0%	0	0%	0
2	3	18	0.18
4	5	29	0.47
6	3	18	0.65
8	1	6	0.71
10	0	0	0.71
12	1	6	0.76
14	1	6	0.82
16	1	6	0.88
18	1	6	0.94
20	0	0	0.94
22	0	0	0.94
24	0	0	0.94
26	1	6	1

is defined here as the entire period between a peak in trading equity and the next *new high* in equity. That means that even drawdowns closely spaced together were separated by *new highs* in profits from the trading combination. That is, the equity curve was still moving up. If there were no break in the drawdown, you'd have a trading combination that was a steady loser or a loser despite occasional wins, and drawdowns would be continuous, not episodic.

Actually, given the probability of being in a drawdown (that is, below the most recent peak in trading profits) almost half the time (46% of the time) and the size/probability relationship in Figure 6–5, what's the realistic probability of starting off with a disastrous sequence? I estimate that with displays like Figure 6–6.

Figure 6–6 shows the actual experience with this trading combination in the white columns. On the right is the 25% drawdown we first noticed in Figure 6–4. Given that one occurrence, I earlier calculated .45 × .06 = .03 or 3% for running into a disaster on day one. However,

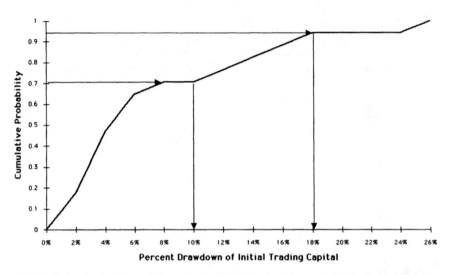

Figure 6–5 Probability of Drawdown. The fourth column in Table 6–1 translates into this picture of the relationship between probability and size of drawdown from adverse runs. This limited experience with the exemplary trading combination suggests that 70% of the drawdowns will be 10% or less before the combination reaches new highs in profitability.

it's apparent from the figure, that there are fewer and fewer drawdowns as we go out further on the x-axis. To estimate the likelihood of a killer drawdown, I fitted through these actual events an exponential (or "growth") curve as a proxy for the actual distribution we cannot know. If we read from it the estimated probabilities, the expected probability for the 25% drawdown is vanishingly small. The probability of a 40% drawdown is surely infinitesimal. This estimate leaves us little excuse to avoid using this particular trading combination.

By displaying the drawdowns experienced in your system testing and applying this straightforward inspection of the results, you can make reasonable estimates of the likelihood of getting hammered right out of the gate.

Significance

The exemplary data used here are of a worst case. This is a trading system with only 30% winners so lots of time is spent in drawdown

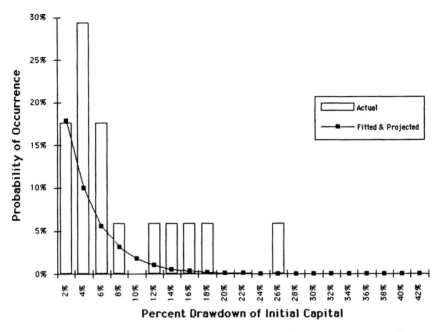

Figure 6–6 Actual and Expected Probability of Drawdown. An exponential curve fitted to the declining frequency of drawdowns suggests vanishingly small probabilities for disastrous 40% drawdowns.

periods. The last analysis assumed that, even though the trading combination was profitable, none of the winnings would be used to support future trading; all drawdowns would be from the initial trading capital. Moreover, drawdowns themselves were (and should be) defined comprehensively and conservatively as the worst reduction in trading equity before a new high in trading equity is set.

Nevertheless, so effective was the use of MAE stops to minimize losses that even lots of losses did not prevent the trader from being around when large winners showed up. Also, the MAE stops prevented any disastrous single loss that would have destroyed the trader.

The loss control from MAE stops also minimized the impact of adverse runs of losses. Figure 6–5 summarizes the actual experience of adverse runs showing how unlikely they would be to break the trader's bank. The significance of losses from adverse runs depends on their distribution. When experience indicates, for instance, that

(1) most adverse runs will cause losses of less than 10%, (2) 95% of the losses will be less than 18% of initial trading capital, and (3) the probability of a trade-stopping 40% drawdown on the most conservative basis is extremely low, heart should be taken and the trading plan executed faithfully.

If examination shows that the probability of hitting the 40% drawdown is high, it's time for revisions. However, that doesn't seem to be common with MAE trading. Consider the probabilities that must occur with even so dismal a system as my 30%-winner example. Using its most common drawdown of 4% (from Figure 6–6) *and* assuming there were no interval of high profits between drawdowns,* it would take ten of these in a row to hit 40% total drawdown. This event would have a probability of $.3^{10} = .0000059$. A 10% drawdown, using the same assumptions, would have, at the worst, a $.06^4 = .00001$ probability. In fact, the evidence collected here shows that lots of small, consecutive losses result in drawdowns that are generally manageable, frequently sizable, and never catastrophic.

Your historical testing may have quite different results and you may set different limits. A 3% chance, a chance that may actually be much lower, of a 25% drawdown moderated by MAE stops is manageable.

IMPACT ON CAMPAIGN TRADING

Campaigning is the overall plan by which the trading manager approaches the market. A campaign is made up of strategies and tactics. For example, strategies could include trading trending and ranging market modes. Tactics could include entry trades, add-on trades, countertrading, and reversal trades. Each one is separately capitalized based on their expected loss on individual trades. Normally, I have advocated risking no more than 2% of total trading capital on any one

---

* This has the effect of turning drawdowns as defined here into independent events so that it would never occur that a drawdown would never be succeeded by another drawdown without an interval of higher profitability. Thus, the fear of succeeding drawdowns is met in these statistics, unless your trading equity actually is headed consistently downward and there is no interval of higher profitability.

trade but, if, for example, add-on trades during a trend had progressed well you might have on at one time:

1. The basic trend entry trade

2. Two or three additional trend add-on trades

3. An add-on day trade. Since this is a day trade, you might avoid your broker seeing a margin requirement but you still have the risk of loss and must account for it by an absorption of capital.

4. A countertrend trade.

I've even seen a situation where a well-developed trend triggered a (brief) ranging trade without ending the trades associated with the trend. In that case, you could add a fifth exposed trade.

In such a situation, you will have some comfort that your trend trades have progressed well (since you now have several of them that were triggered by earlier successes) and add-on trades usually have a very high percentage of success. Since the returns to any individual tactic are largely independent of those of another tactic, diversification effects usually work in your favor by offsetting losses in one tactic with wins in another.

Nevertheless, correlation between tactics should be checked where it's conceivable and it is possible that several could go bad coincidentally. Though you could check past experience on this one, the correlation of trading system/tradable combinations is usually pretty sporadic. Where you do find relationships are those well-established among stock industries, groups and sectors; indices; and futures related to underlying economic sectors (the rate complex, currencies, indices of many kinds).

What you must check is whether, once a trading system's entries and exits are used on a specific pair of tradables, the correlation events survives and, after trade management (i.e., stops), any correlation of returns and drawdown experiences survives. If the trading systems for the two (or more) related tradables are different, correlation of returns and drawdowns is even more problematic.

Moreover, using standard statistics for this comparison is inadequate. Since, in statistical terms, gains and losses occur episodically, correlations may be very low when measured in the usual way. It's

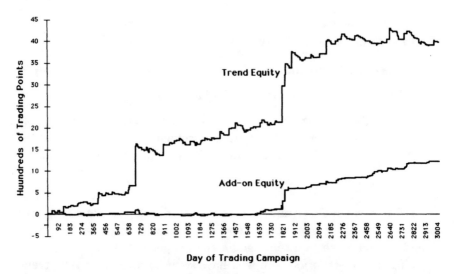

Figure 6–7   Equity for Two Trading Tactics. Since drawdowns and advances occur episodically during trading campaigns, visual comparisons are more to the point in searching for relationships between those events in two different trading tactics. Here, the equity curve for simple the trend trading of Figure 6–1 is compared to that for additional day-trades taken during trend trades.

better to inspect the behavior of the equity curve visually, comparing the fluctuations of two combinations directly for sympathetic movement. Finding such movement, you then have the problem of determining if there exists a relationship and, if so, whether the relationship is likely to be in force in the future.

For example, Figure 6–7 compares the equity lines for two different trading tactics. The "Trend Equity" line is the trend trading first seen in Figure 6–1; the second is that for add-on day trades* taken during the first period's trend trades. That the add-on trades would be related to the trend trades is built in to their rationale, yet looking at the two lines suggests that there is not necessarily a close relationship. In fact, the correlation between the two is .26.

---

* The trading rule, outlined in *Campaign Trading!,* applies but when, during a long trend trade, the low of the day is below the 20-day average, closing the position on the close of the day. If short, sell if the high exceeds the 20-day average and buy it back on the close of the same day.

The episodic nature of the relationship of two trading combinations plays out well here. For roughly half of the 11 years shown here, the add-on trades did not do well while the trend trading tactic advanced steadily in equity. Add-ons did not participate in the single large gain around the 700th trade day nor did they participate in the trend trades' gains from many small trades taken during the first six years. Then, in 1989, around the 1600th day, the tactic started to work well with very few drawdowns. During that same period, the trend equity line did advance, but had several periods of significant drawdown.

Experiences like these—where the tradable is the same and the trading tactics somewhat related—generally produce very little relationship in equity impacts. I am tempted to say "never" because I haven't seen a solid relationship, but they still are possible. Nevertheless, I don't believe this concern is worth more than this visual inspection. By the time you have differences in the tradables, differences in the trading tactics, and differences in the loss management techniques, you have very little relationship between the equity curves. I certainly can't prove they don't exist, but I couldn't find one to show you!

Correlated Equity Curves

Where you did find those strings of losses from different trading combinations coincided regularly, you deal with the issue by raising the capital available, lowering the amount of loss acceptable on trades (tough to do if you've selected the right MAE stop level to start with), reducing the number of contracts used by each tactic (only possible if your MAE analysis allows you to trade more than one contract within the 2% of capital limit), or ceasing one of the two related tactics.

The best example of this is trading the same tactic on highly related tradables, for example, the DMark and the Swiss Franc. The correlation in monthly returns between these two using, as an example, the Donchian Rule, was reported to be on the order of .77 in 1993. (Kestner, Lars. "The Role of Diversification," *Technical Analysis of Stocks and Commodities,* March, 1996.) in 1993. The simple thing to do is trade the more liquid issue in greater size since you're getting the same movement in both and diversification benefits are minimized if you trade two vehicles with highly correlated equity curves.

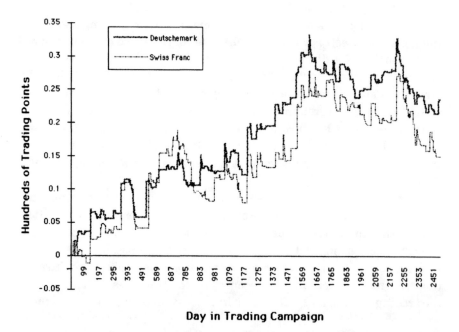

Figure 6–8 Trading Related Tradables. When the DMark and Swiss are traded with the same trading system, the numbers come out slightly different but the relationship between the equity curves is apparent. Trading highly correlated vehicles with the same tactics robs the trader of the benefits of diversification.

Take Figure 6–8 as an example. Here, both the Swiss Franc and Deutschemark contracts are traded with the same dual moving average system used in Figure 6–1, albeit with 12- and 20-day parameters for the averages. The Swiss contract came out less favorably, but both advances and declines were shared coincidentally. Indeed, the correlation of the two equity curves is an astoundingly high .94. Here is clearly a case where trading both doubles the downside.

Kestner reports the correlation of returns for Deutschemark and Japanese Yen at .38 (Figure 6–9) and that for Deutschemark and Gold at −.01 (Figure 6–10), roughly half that of the Swiss Franc. The equivalent figures for the equity of the dual moving average system are .59 for the DM/JY and −.27 for DM/Gold. The DM/Y relation is clearly less sympathetic than DM/Swiss and both head in the same general upward direction.

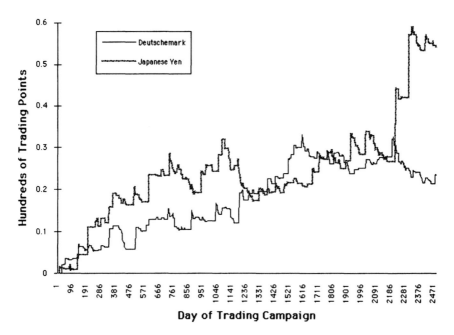

Figure 6-9 Deutschemark and Yen. Traded with the same system used in Figure 6-8, the relationship between these two major currencies shifts in and out of phase. Drawdowns sometimes appear coincidently and sometimes opposed.

Drawdowns seem barely related. Looking at DM/Gold, it's hard to see any relationship unless, as the correlation suggests, it is negative.

Combining, for purposes of exposition, the several curves gives Figure 6-11 which, in turn, gives us the drawdown chart in Figure 6-12.* This sobering presentation shows, for exposition purposes only, drawdown effects that would certainly get any trader's attention. Though the general direction is upward, gold's huge fluctuations impose drawdowns on the total that are relatively large, generally diminishing the normal diversification smoothing of returns. To boot, gold's losses in the latter part of the period drag down the overall results of the portfolio, only slightly offset by the Yen's gains.

---

* The more proper procedure would be to adjust the ratios of contracts to achieve a consistent dollar exposure between all four combinations.

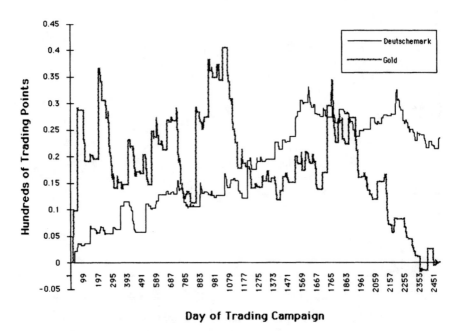

Figure 6–10   Deutschemark and Gold. Trading gold with the same system as in Figures 6–8 and 6–9 actually generates a negative relationship, −.27. Trading a pair such as this could potentially smooth overall returns if both had positive results. (The two curves have been mean-centered for exposition.)

A look at Figure 6–12 to see what our expectation of disaster is confirms that drawdown is frequent and steadily runs in the 10% to 15% range. Gains, while strong, are short-lived and most of the trading period is spent in drawdown from previous peaks. Some of the drawdown periods last over a year and a half as hard-won equity is worn away by various combinations' individual losses. Though the chance of hitting a 40% overall reduction in the capital committed to all four trading combinations appears low, drawdown periods happen quite frequently.

Since each trading combination is separately capitalized and none individually come close to a trading cutoff (though Gold is working on it), the trader's consolation is that overall gains for the Portfolio of four are greater than trading any one issue alone. At the close

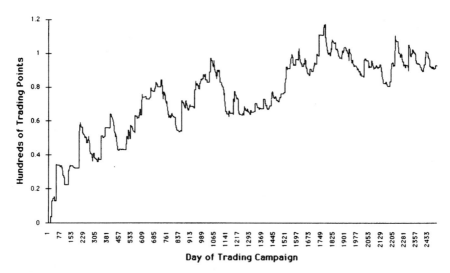

Figure 6-11 Combining Trading Combinations. Melding the results of the figures above for Deutschemark, Swiss Franc, Yen, and Gold generates this jagged curve. Though the direction is upward, drawdowns seem to be serious. For a better look at those, see Figure 6–12.

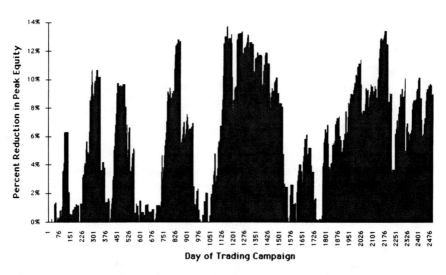

Figure 6-12 Drawdowns from Four Combinations. Somewhat easier to see are the drawdowns, presented here as a percentage reduction from peak equity plus initial trading capital.

Table 6–2   Variability of Returns. DMark, Swiss, Yen, and the total portfolio achieve a K-ratio > 1 but fail to make the grade when the risk-free interest rate is included via the Sharpe ratio. Only the Yen, with its
last-minute surge, achieves profitability in excess of the risk free rate.

	DMark	Swiss	Yen	Gold	Total Portfolio
K-ratio	2.13	1.43	1.42	−0.51	1.60
Std dev./avg.	0.48	0.51	0.50	0.50	0.31
Sharpe ratio	−2.41	−3.22	−1.19	−11.74	−0.90

of the period, DMarks are up $23,500, Swiss $15,500, Yen $54,900,
and Gold $0 (Table 6–2).

Next you check the variability in relation to return with the
K-ratio and the Sharpe ratio which are in Table 6–2.* The K-ratio
test favors a steady advance of the equity curve and the author, Lars
Kestner, recommends a minimum value of one for a single trading combination. Save gold, all achieve this but the group does not achieve the
higher hurdle of 3.0 for a portfolio.

Also, despite overall profitability, these trading combinations are
generally disappointing when faced with the job of earning a return in
excess of the risk free rate. Variability of the returns in terms of the
average return is fairly low and reduced further in the total portfolio,
surprising given the steep drawdowns seen in the equity curve but
consistent with the larger total profitability. It's apparent that all the
loss management in the world can't make a humdrum system sufficiently profitable even if it can prevent disasters.

---

* Kestner, Lars, "Measuring System Performance," *Technical Analysis of Stocks and
Commodities* (March, 1996) pp. 46–50. The K-ratio compares the slope of a regression
line of the combination's equity curve to its standard error to reward closeness of fit
to the line of advance.

$$\text{K-ratio} = \text{Slope of regression} / [(\text{Standard error of slope})(\text{Number of observations})^{1/2}]$$

Sharpe, William, "Mutual Fund Performance," *Journal of Business* (January, 1966),
pp. 119–138. The Sharpe ratio is the excess return divided by the standard deviation
of return.

$$\text{Sharpe ratio} = (\text{Return} - \text{Risk free rate})/\text{Standard deviation of return}$$

The bottom line for this analysis:

1. The tiny portfolio is susceptible to drawdowns somewhat higher than the 4% to 8% seen for DMarks alone but nothing so high as 25%.

2. The potential for disastrous 40% reductions in equity appears minimal.

3. Diversification benefits for this oddly-correlated group (Swiss and DMarks highly correlated, Yen somewhat correlated, Gold negatively correlated) appear only in the reduction of worst case drawdowns of equity from the 25% level to the 10% level.

4. Profitability vs. the risk free rate is inadequate so its must be inadequate in comparison to other risky strategies (say, a stock index fund).

IMPACT ON BETTING STRATEGIES

Betting strategies alter the size of the amount traded based on, commonly, the likelihood of success, pyramiding, the progression of betting, and the amount of capital available. Of all these, the last two have some theoretical and experiential support. Increasing or decreasing the number of shares or contracts based on capital available is straightforward: the size of the play for an individual trading tactic is simply limited by the 2% rule, the loss being defined by an MAE stop. As your capital grows (hopefully), 2% of it grows apace and the size of your commitments grows with it.

It's the use of progressions that's more difficult. An individual trading tactic certainly produces a series of wins and losses (outcomes) that resembles a betting series and a properly prepared progression will eventually win. The trouble with progressions is that a run of losses can extend the trading beyond your capability to play. In Chapter 7, I give some examples (and references) for using progressions in trading and show how your experience with runs of losses can impact this particular betting strategy.

SUMMARY

Practical inspection of the day-to-day performance of individual trading combinations and that of the group of combinations as a whole will give a good indication of the potential for disastrous hits. Asset allocation schemes can be used by quantitatively-oriented trading management to objectively assemble portfolios of trading combinations (or traders, for that matter) but those after a graphic depiction of their potential to lose may use the approach outlined here. Repeated experience, as shown in the graphics, may lend some intuitive understanding of the nature of the drawdowns faced day-to-day that a smoothly assembled efficient frontier does not.

7

MARTINGALES

If the runs information means anything, it means there will be adverse runs. Runs of winners are fine, but we'll be faced with losers certainly, especially as I've defined runs for trading purposes in this book. If you recall that definition is that an adverse run lasts until a new high in equity is achieved, even if there are some intervening wins. Is there some means of taking advantage of this situation?

Given enough money, almost anything can be overcome, even adverse runs. With adequate capital (i.e., *LOTS* of capital), you can adjust the size of your bets to suit a variety of win/loss sequences. An extraordinary amount of capital is needed because you don't know how long the adversity will persist. The trick is estimating that length and size probabilistically and arranging your capital to withstand it. Fortunately, with MAE stops, loss size is controlled and the major remaining question is how long adversity will go on. In the previous section, we went over the estimation of adversity from runs by examining the experience both for a single trading combination and for a group of trading combinations.

There is another tactic though. Ferguson, Eliason, and Pelletier* have dealt with the subject of handling a series of trades through "betting" strategies. The technique, a *martingale,* adjusts the bet size by fixed rules following a win or loss. In Ferguson's first article, he demonstrated the positive impact this approach can have on the typical trend following trading system, turning it from a loser to a winner. The approach was so apt I applied it to the humdrum system discussed in this book. That system is a small winner in DMarks, Swiss, and Yen, but a loser in gold (or, at best, a small winner).

Martingales are best suited for professional traders and trading organizations who are not only well-capitalized but also thoroughly disciplined. It can be a disastrous strategy from which to exit in midstream so, given that quitting a strategy prematurely is common among individual traders, it's not something unseasoned traders should undertake.

Moreover, if applied to a series of trades that take place over two or three years, even a institutional trader may have difficulty implementing it simply because normal turnover on the trading floor will mean he or she won't be there in two or three years. In a well-organized and disciplined institution with adequate position tracking facilities, "run control" or "loss management" techniques can be successfully implemented over longer periods of time. Even there, though, it helps if the trading combination used trades rather frequently so that traders and management can see the technique working and get away from the notion that they are sitting on a loss which can only be requited at some distant time in the future.

One factor in trading that favors a martingale is that winning trades are normally larger than losing trades. Although this isn't the

---

* Ferguson, James W., "Martingales," *Stocks & Commodities,* V. 8:2 (Seattle, 1988) pp. 56–59, and "Reverse Martingales V. 8:3 (Seattle, 1988) pp. 105–108.

Eliason, Peter "Tactical Stock Trading," *Stocks & Commodities,* V. 7:3 (Seattle, 1988) pp. 69–72.

Pelletier, Robert, "Martingale Money Management," *Stocks & Commodities,* V. 6:7 (Seattle, 1988) pp. 265–267.

case for every instance, traders normally pick systems where a 2:1 or 3:1 ratio is maintained between the size of a win and the size of a loss. Were this not so, trading a martingale would be very tedious so you may go through ten trades only to eventually win an amount equal to your average win.

Lastly, transactions costs are a big factor in using martingales. Unlike casinos, exchanges and brokers charge for their services irrespective of outcomes. Transactions costs must be very low to keep them from being a material detriment to the ultimate outcome. All these factors play a part in the exemplary analysis shown in this chapter.

Before going into the simulation using the crude data on which this book focuses, here's a brief description of simple and complex martingales for those who aren't familiar with them. The origins of the name seem lost in time. It seems certain though that, contrary to legend, there was never anyone named Martingale. Ferguson felt the term originated from the French describing an apparatus used to keep a horse from swinging its head—a reference to the use of martingales to check losses.

SIMPLE MARTINGALE

A simple martingale consists of this rule: Double your bet (at even odds) after each loss until you win. When you finally win, your winnings will amount to your original bet. In a trading situation, that means that your expected win is the same size as your expected loss. For example, check this sequence:

Trade	Bet	Win or Loss	Equity
1	$1,000	Loss	$(1,000)
2	2,000	Loss	(3,000)
3	4,000	Loss	(7,000)
4	8,000	Win	1,000

Try a few sequences of your own. The bet size (the number of shares or contracts) increases rapidly (from $8,000 to $16,000 to $32,000, to $64,000 and upward) so that you run the chance of running out of money. MAE stops help with this by limiting the size of the loss which, in trading terms, is really the size of your bet. If the same sequence as above were played out with the stop of $310, things would be more manageable for most traders, though the commitment rises faster than most would like. Again, it's assumed the win will be $310 just as will be the loss:

Trade	Bet	Win or Loss	Equity
1	$ 310	Loss	$ (310)
2	620*	Loss	(930)
3	1,240	Loss	(2,170)
4	2,480	Win	310

* Two contracts with a stop at 31 ticks from entry.

Whether this would be economic tactic depends on the frequency of the trading combination's trading, the transactions costs (15 trades at $19 costs costs $285), the length of time it takes for the sequence of trades to play out, on average, the returns on alternative trading techniques, and tax rates.

COMPLEX MARTINGALE

As easy as the simple martingale is to understand, the complex martingales are not. There are many varieties of complex martingales but all have one feature: They reduce the size of the additional bets that must be made at the cost of extending the time you spend in the betting sequence.

To see a complex martingale (again, just one of many possible) working consider what would happen if, in the above sequence, you bet not double the previous bet but only one unit more or less:

| | | Win or | | |
Trade	Bet	Loss	Loss/Gain	Equity
1	$ 310	Loss	$ (310)	$ (310)
2	620*	Loss	(620)	(930)
3	930	Loss	(930)	(1,860)
4	1,240	Win	1,240	(620)
5	930	Win	930	310

* Two contracts. Share traders could adjust the number of shares, commission costs allowing.

The result was the same but it took longer to get it. Again, you should try a few of these sequences yourself. Just for a taste of a complex martingale the rules for the number of contracts to trade were, after the first loss, to add the number of contracts traded in the loss to the sequence of trades, sum the first and last number in the sequence, and trade that number next. If a trade is a winner, strike the first and last numbers in the sequence and sum the remaining first and last numbers to get the number to trade next. For example:

| | | Number to | Win or |
Trade	Sequence	Trade	Loss
1	1	1	Loss
2	1,1*	1 + 1 = 2	Loss
3	1,1*,2	1 + 2 = 3	Loss
4	1,1*,2,3	1 + 3 = 4	Win
5	1*,2	1 + 2 = 3	Win

* Marks the second "1" in the series.

You can readily imagine with all the combinations of wins and losses the market can throw at you how complicated a series could be generated. To really get a practical feel for this, you should play with the martingale simulation given in Appendix J. You'll quickly see that, even though martingales come right in the end, you'll not enjoy a situation where the win size is equal to the loss size. Figure 7–1 is

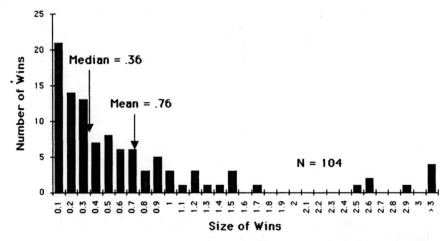

Figure 7–1   Distribution of Win Size. Computed for the trend following dual moving average system used throughout this book, the distribution highlights that selecting an appropriate wins size for martingale modeling is subject to wide latitude.

an example from Appendix J where you can also read an explanation of the columns and their computations in Table 7–1.

Hitting six losses in a row is not that frequent but when it happens you'll need a while to recover. In this simulation, the martingale gradually wore away the $6,510 loss that had been built up at the start of the series but it took it eleven more trades to get back to just $310 in winnings. Many traders who have prayed fervently to get back to breakeven might think this a good result but would they have stayed the course through 17 trades?

In Table 7–1, P(Win) = .5 and the ratio of the win size to the loss size is just 1:1. Given that you have a higher win ratio or a better win:loss ratio, things can be much better despite adverse runs of losses. Table 7–2 shows an adverse run with P(win) = .4 and wins:losses = 3.0.

I leave it to you to experiment with the model in the appendix but it turns out that selecting a system with the right dollar win:loss ratio is most important to managing a martingale, especially for a trading combination that doesn't have a good probability of winning, as most don't. Of the things you can influence in designing and selecting your trading combination, you may have little control over the

Table 7-1 Long Drawdown. Though martingales can always bring one back to new highs in profitability, a truly adverse run of trades absorbs both time and capital.

Assumptions:		P(WIN) 0.5	$Win / $ Loss 1		Bet Size $310		
Trade	Bet	Win or Loss	Contracts Loss/Gain	Equity Units	Equity		Bet Table
1	1	Loss	−1	−1	$ (310)	−45	10
2	2	Loss	−2	−3	(930)	−36	9
3	3	Loss	−3	−6	(1,860)	−28	8
4	4	Loss	−4	−10	(3,100)	−27	8
5	5	Loss	−5	−15	(4,650)	−21	7
6	6	Loss	−6	−21	(6,510)	−20	10
7	7	Win	7	−14	(4,340)	−19	8
8	6	Win	6	−8	(2,480)	−15	6
9	6	Loss	−6	−14	(4,340)	−14	6
10	6	Win	6	−8	(2,480)	−11	8
11	6	Win	6	−2	(620)	−10	5
12	3	Loss	−3	−5	(1,550)	−9	5
13	4	Win	4	−1	(310)	−8	6
14	2	Loss	−2	−3	(930)	−6	4
15	3	Loss	−3	−6	(1,860)	−5	4
16	4	Win	4	−2	(620)	−4	5
17	3	Win	3	1	310	−3	3
18	0	False	0	1	310	−2	3
19	0	False	0	1	310	−1	2
20	0	False	0	1	310	0	1

Table 7-2 Adverse Runs. A good win size compared to the loss size (the MAE stop) can overcome a multitude of bad trades, even an adverse win probability. A martingale series is terminated when the equity after a trade turns positive.

Assumptions:		P(WIN) 0.4	$ Win / $ Loss 3		Bet Size $310
Trade	Bet	Win or Loss	Contracts Loss/Gain	Equity Units	Equity
1	1	Loss	−1	−1	$ (310)
2	2	Loss	−2	−3	(930)
3	3	Loss	−3	−6	(1,860)
4	4	Loss	−4	−10	(3,100)
5	5	Win	15	5	1,550

ratio of wins and losses without imposing too many rules and overfitting. Small adjustments, however, often effect the size of you wins and losses and, in MAE, you have an excellent tool for managing the size of your losses.

Managing the size of the wins is tougher. The average win figure is not necessarily a good one as the size of the wins is usually quite skewed (see Figure 7–1).

Nor is the distribution of loss size normal. See Figure 7–2.

Thus, it isn't idle to inspect closely the distribution of the size of wins and losses. When you actually trade, remember, you won't get average wins or losses but values all over the ballpark, usually within expected ranges. Thus, you must plan to go through many martingales to come up with the average win and average loss, assuming prior experience holds true. Some experimenting with the models will give you a feel for the levers available to you but the most common result of low frequency trading is to cut things too finely: without a lot of trades, the win size and loss size tend toward the median rather than the mean. As a result, the ratio of win size to loss size moves closer to 1:1 from the ideal 2:1 or 3:1. In the example above, using means we

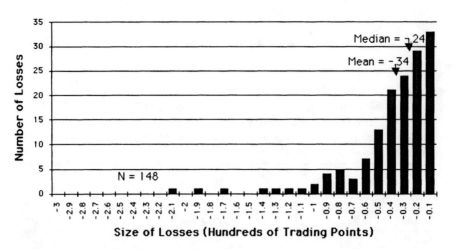

Figure 7–2 Distribution of Loss Size. Just as wins aren't normally distributed, neither are losses. Consider, though, the combined distributions about the breakeven point are near to normal with the exception of the winners' long tail to the right. Losses can be controlled with well-defined MAE stops.

have .76/.34 = 2 while if medians are used we have .36/.24 = 1.5. The practical result is that, if you're going to use martingales you need to use them for a lot of trades to get sufficient to reach your desired win-size, loss-size ratio.

In summary, martingales should be used with a trading tactic that trades frequently (add-on day trades come to mind), where the probability of profit is 40% or better and/or the ratio of win size to loss size is better than 2:1, to pick rough rules of thumb. These factors shorten the length of the martingale which will cut down the number of trades before conclusion which, in turn, reduces the cost of capital invested in the tactic as well as commissions and slippage. Given that the martingale only returns the size of the original "bet" times the win size:loss size ratio, careful comparison, considering the amount of capital tied up (losses plus margin), to alternative speculations should be made. Keeping in mind that transactions will be numerous, tax effects must also be added to the mix. Dealers with the advantage on all these issues will probably find martingales of most use.

MARTINGALES ON CRUDE OIL

As an example, consider the crude oil trading described in *Campaign Trading!* and elaborated here. To apply a martingale to this trading campaign, I selected the complex martingale from Appendix J, elaborated for the longer loss strings experienced when only 30% of the trades are winners. When no martingale was in progress and a win was recorded, equity went up by the amount of the win or down by the amount of the MAE stop if it were hit.* If a martingale wasn't in progress and a loss came up, the martingale began with the recording of a loss.

To track the martingale in a trading situation means keeping track of the counts for wins and losses, but also the actual amounts won or lost on each trade. In this application to crude, the martingale was

---

* For those who haven't read *Campaign Trading!*, MAE stops are developed on trading combinations which have an entry and and exit defined, without consideration of stops. Therefore, it's possible for the combination to record a win but, later, after imposition of a stop, to have that win turned to a loss because, during the trade, the adverse excursion exceeded the MAE stop.

ended whenever the martingale's count of outstanding values was equal to or greater than zero or the martingale's actual dollar winnings were equal to or greater than zero. That is, even if the martingale's count had not played itself out fully, achieving a new high in equity would stop the trading series.

In Table 7–3, the first column shows the number of share blocks or contracts traded, in this case, one for the first loss in the third row, two in the 18th row and so on. The second column totals the number of contracts or share blocks lost as the martingale progresses. In this excerpted martingale, it was down ten contracts before winning on a five-contract trade in the last row. Column 3 sums the trading points lost or gained by the martingale as it progresses. In crude, $310 = 31 trading points at $10 each, usually displayed as ".31." Normally, only the last value will be positive, but not always. See below. Lastly, column four accumulates the tradings wins and losses to form the equity curve.

Under these conditions you may not end the martingale with a profit! It's possible to have a combination of wins and losses which end the martingale series but at the same time experience a combination of win sizes and loss sizes which end the martingale with a loss. For example, if the first trade is a loss of .31, the next trade will be two contracts or blocks of shares. If that trade wins .12, then you have ended the martingale but your profit is (2 Contracts × 12 Points/Contract) − 31 Points = −7 Points. In this eleven year series, this happened nine times, the losses ranging from 15 points to 78 points with, as we shall see, very little impact on the outcome. Here are the actual points lost: 25, 78, 29, 62, 15, 7, 56, 38, 7. In eleven years, 41 martingale series were counted.

In practice, all this works out to steeper equity drawdowns than trading without using the martingale and extremely quick, explosive recoveries to new highs. The martingale progression served to increase the volatility of returns and, in the process, generate profits two or three times the size of the same series of trades without martingale money management. Figure 7–3 shows the two equity curves together, the first the dual-moving average trend trading system and the second the same system with martingale money management.

Figure 7–3 shows the results of combining MAE stops with martingale money management. The Trend Equity line is the dual moving

Table 7-3 Exemplary Martingale Worksheet. A trading martingale must track both the martingale's counts of trades won or lost but also the actual amount won or lost on each trade, here, by trade in the third column and cumulatively in the fourth column. (This is just the beginning of a long martingale.)

Number Blocks Won or Lost	Martingale's Blocks Outstanding	Martingale Equity	Trend and Martingale Equity
False	False	False	112.77
False	False	False	112.77
False	False	False	112.77
−1	−1	−0.31	112.46
−1	−1	−0.31	112.46
−1	−1	−0.31	112.46
−1	−1	−0.31	112.46
−1	−1	−0.31	112.46
−1	−1	−0.31	112.46
−1	−1	−0.31	112.46
−1	−1	−0.31	112.46
−1	−1	−0.31	112.46
−1	−1	−0.31	112.46
−1	−1	−0.31	112.46
−1	−1	−0.31	112.46
−1	−1	−0.31	112.46
−2	−3	−0.93	111.84
−2	−3	−0.93	111.84
−3	−6	−1.86	110.91
−3	−6	−1.86	110.91
−3	−6	−1.86	110.91
−3	−6	−1.86	110.91
−3	−6	−1.86	110.91
−4	−10	−2.58	110.19
−4	−10	−2.58	110.19
−4	−10	−2.58	110.19
5	−5	−2.43	110.34

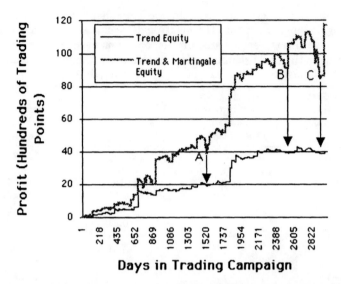

Figure 7–3 Explosive Results of Martingale Management. Managing the same series of trades with a martingale system produces explosive results at the cost of increased volatility. Drawdown B had an 1–11 win-loss streak before recovering and Drawdown C went 3–20 before recovering it all on just one trade and going on to new highs in profitability.

average system using an MAE stop of .31. The only thing that changed in the other line was the use of the martingale system. The result was to triple overall profits at the expense of increased volatility of returns and greater commitment of capital.

Ignoring for the moment the dramatic movement around C, notice that at A and B, downturns in the Trend Equity line became major dips in the martingale line. On the other hand, the slope of the martingale line is much steeper upward. This is because, absent extended drawdowns, the 2:1 win/loss ratio of this trading combination and the MAE stops holding losses to .31 mean, together with the growth in contracts as the martingale progressed, meant that just one win would overcome all the previous losses.

To say it another way, MAE kept the losses small until a solid win came along, a win which was amplified by the greater number of contracts being traded when it popped up. Thus, the sharp upthrusts in the Trend Equity line were amplified in the martingale line. A big win when you're running a martingale with a good dollar win/loss ratio is a very big win indeed.

Along with the increased volatility and higher profit came higher capital commitments. Though profits easily funded the drawdowns, had the worst come first, a loss series of 3,000 points ($30,000 would have been endured up front, something most managements could not stomach). Additionally, the margin required to support these positions lowers the return to capital. Figure 7–4 shows how the margin requirements shift with the invocation of the martingale sequences during drawdown periods.

Margin required rises dramatically in the last drawdown where as many as 28 contracts must be supported for what started as a single-contract trade. This is meant for large money or large lines of credit. However, most of the time, requirements are much less and the computation of return to capital will be more favorable.

Taken together, this exemplary analysis nicely demonstrates the strengths and weaknesses of the martingale strategy. On the favorable

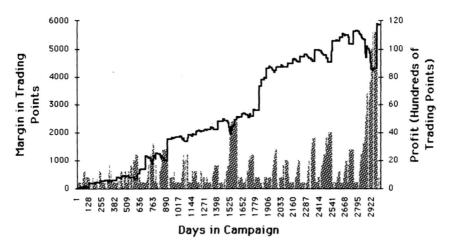

Figure 7–4 Martingale Margin Requirements. Margin pops dramatically as the martingale sequences elongate. Margins are the columnar elements of the chart while profits are the line element. Note the differing scales.

tally, there is the significant increase in profitability, an increase
which would be even more dramatic with a system that hit, say, 50%
of its trades correctly or had a more consistent win size − loss size
ratio. The unfavorable tally includes the great increase in volatility,
experienced as larger drawdowns and long (not longer) periods of adversity before winning through. There are no perfect solutions in trading, just tradeoffs between risk and return. Martingales are no
exception and analyses like these will help the trading manager make
the implementation decision.

8

TRADING MANAGEMENT

While we are certainly far from true control of trading activity for relatively assured profits, it's not too early to consider how that might work. It's reasonable to think of this because we can put a measure to losses which is part of giving us a standard for performance (the other half being measures of gain which have been well studied). We actually have a picture of how a particular trading combination should perform; we know, to some degree, what constitutes normal experiences and what doesn't; and, since we know what the losses should be, we have the gain/loss picture more firmly focused.

PORTFOLIO IMPACTS

Though I've used the gain/loss terminology, portfolio managers will immediately think of risk/return. Those who assemble portfolios efficiently, portfolios which include speculative trading combinations, will recognize that the limitation of losses alters the risk profile of the trading asset which, if done across the board, means a shift in the composition and weightings of their portfolio. Trading combinations using MAE stops generally should have lower variance of returns but,

as seen in Chapter 7, combinations using progressive capital commitment schemes (betting progressions) may have both higher returns
and higher variance of returns. All of this necessitates a portfolio re-
assessment.

DAY-TO-DAY TRADING

On the more practical day-to-day level, trading by system using MAE
techniques should be more manageable than trading until the system
taps out or it's time for the end-of-the-year wrapup. After all, management is a specific discipline. Without going into all the ways it's
been defined, list the specific things managers do. Managers:

- Study an issue to reach a goal.

- Prepare or plan a course of action to reach the goal.

- Predict from their plan a desired result.

- Direct the execution of their plan.

- Monitor and/or measure deviations from the desired result.

- Correct their plan.

Managers are always in the loop of measuring results, seeing deviations from plan and making corrections to the plan (Figure 8–1).
Traders, in contrast, are usually wondering if there's been a change in
plan. "I took a loss," they mull. "Was it a serious loss? Is it telling me
something? Did I do something wrong? Has the situation changed? Did
everyone else do something wrong? Am I out of touch? What happened?"
   Traders usually think they have a plan when what they have is
an idea of how to get into a trade. Someone one level up who's managing traders usually hasn't any illusions that he's "planning, direct-
ing, and controlling." He tries to make sure the cannons are firing
regularly and pointedly rather than rolling around aimlessly.
   Instead, what if the trader could turn to his plan and check if the
loss was within expected size or if the overall frequency of losses was
within expected ranges? What if wins were similarly comparable to

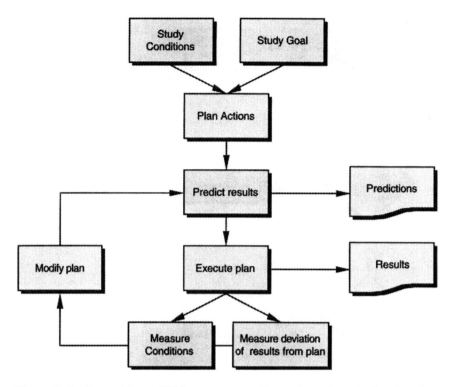

Figure 8–1 Control Loop. While managers achieve planned results by changing their plan as deviations crop up, traders usually have no way of knowing if their failures are normal or abnormal. Traders have no means of making corrections toward a goal. It's impossible to manage trading without the means to assess the situation objectively.

plan? For a trader, a simple checklist would then tell him if he were performing properly (Figure 8–2).

Here's another thought: a trading manager who knows objectively what his traders' losses should look like (as most trading managers feel intuitively) has a tool for making changes. He can look at losses first through the checklist above to identify problems with the trader, problems with conditions, or problems with trading rules (Figure 8–3).

To make these assessments, either at the trader's level or the manager's level, some standard is necessary. To say whether a trader

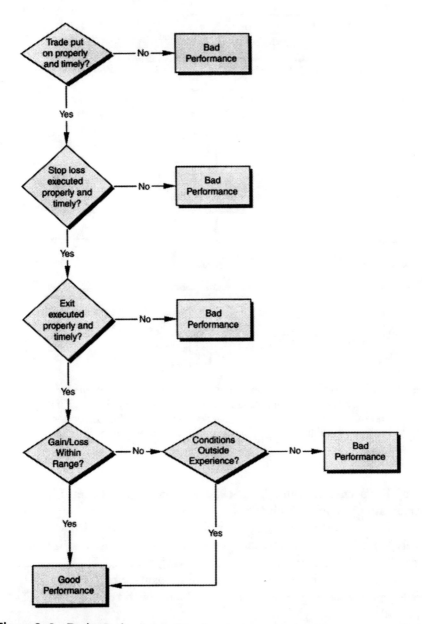

Figure 8–2 Trader Performance. Broad categories of judgment tell the trader or his manager if he or she is performing to spec. There should be no distress for a loss taken properly but there should be distress for a win taken improperly.

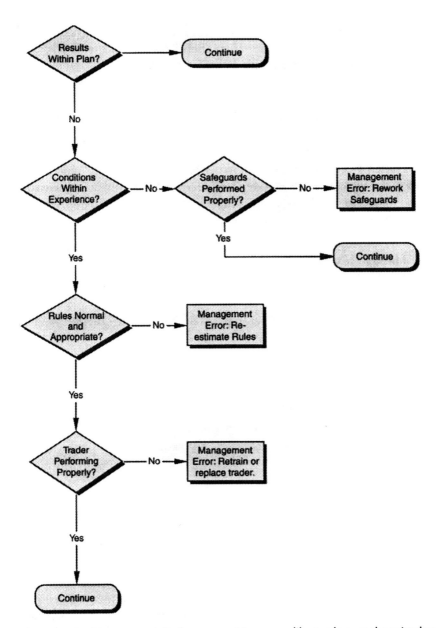

Figure 8–3 Management Performance. Managers, like traders, make mistakes. When results are out of bounds, adverse excursion measurements provide objective means of assessing where the problem is.

was early or late in getting out of a bad trade, you must know where the stop level should have been. If you believe the stop varies with the trade, the conditions of the market, or the ability of the trader you have a lot of variables to deal with and none you can cite without arbitrariness. If, on the other hand, you set the stops based on the elements you can control—the entry point, your indicators, and your rules—there's a good chance you'll find a distinct stop (and/or reversal) point to which you can manage.

Notice I said "manage." Knowing your "wrong point" objectively gives you a beacon when you drift off course. Correct to the target as a good manager would. Knowing your historical win profitability and choosing your loss level you should be able to

- Manage losses: size, frequency, runs. Isn't there a better term than "runs" for the phenomenon of losses occurring in a row and depleting capital?

- Manage precious trading capital by determining what level is needed for each set of rules.

- Manage trading rules and systems by loss/gain targets.

- Manage your traders, measuring by whether they performed the system they were charged to perform.

- Manage speculative portfolios allocating your capital, people, and systems by better-defined loss/gain targets.

ELABORATIONS

Typical Path

This book has focused on adverse excursion because it is most important to manage losing properly. However, back in Chapter 2, definitions of two forms of favorable excursion were also given. These two definitions serve when defining what could be called the *typical path* of a trade. Like adverse excursion, excursion analysis of winning trades begins with separating the winners from the losers, the winning behavior from the losing behavior. These excursions are then analyzed with an eye to finding operational regularity, behaviors that can be used in the management of the winning trade. Some of this was touched on in *Campaign Trading!* where the ideas of add-on trades and reversal trades were described as well as the subject of moving up stops. Just as the general question for adverse price movement is "How far against us do winners go?" the symmetrical question for favorable excursion is often "How little for us do winners go?"

Redefining Winners and Losers

Another analytical area that's sometimes fruitful is questioning what a winner and a loser is. In this book, it's been simply defined as a profitable or unprofitable trade. However, there may well be a middle zone between winning and losing, an area plus or minus n points from the entry where you've got a draw. Perhaps it's defined by transactions costs, perhaps by required return (somewhere between losing money outright and not making enough to justify this trade over some other). In this approach, you separate trades into three groups and see if behavior after entry is markedly different.

Related Indicators

The conjoint events (trading signal: excursion measurement) that MAE analysis uses could have been other events. For example, if you trade the S&P from short-term money flows or exchange rates from short term rate differentials, it would be legitimate to compare price excursion, favorable and adverse, from your "signal" in the underlying indicator. Nothing in the technique described here restricts the trading rules to price-based numbers.

Using Closes

MAE uses price extremes, normally highs and lows, but it's occasionally fruitful to use closes instead of extremes as the measure. Highs and lows are thinly traded and, sometimes, not really traded at all while closes are difficult to trade on a stop basis. However, where liquidity is bare, the close might be the most likely price to actually receive or take. Too, its excursions are generally less than those of the high or low so that you get less adversity to handle at the cost of increased intraday vigilance and some premium for efficient execution at the close.

CONCLUSION

All these elaborations stem from knowing what losses "should" look like. That knowledge gives you the tool to control losses so the wins can do their work. There are more than enough traders and trading rules to generate winning trades but there are few objective techniques for managing losses appropriately. This book described one such practical technique: measuring maximum adverse excursion.

Appendix A

COMPUTING MAE

Maximum Adverse Excursion is defined and explained in Chapter 2. This Appendix provides Microsoft Excel 4.0 code* which can be used as is or modified to fit your own needs.

The worksheet is structured in rows, each row representing a unit of time, usually one day.

Begin by loading Date, Open, High, Low and Close in the first five columns, columns A, B, C, D, and E.

Next, in column F, indicate the position outstanding at the close of the day. This value is a +1 for a long position, 0 for no position, and −1 for a short position.

Any value will serve as a logical "switch" that columns to the right can use for computation. The position column can be computed or simply put in manually. If elaborate computations must be made, additional columns can be inserted before this column to handle them. In this example, the values have simply been inserted.

Next, record the price of the position taken. In cell G2 enter an initialization value of zero. In cell G3, enter

$$=IF(F2< >F3,IF(F3=1,-E3,IF(F3=-1,E3,0)),G2)$$

---

* Microsoft has been good to date about compatibility between various versions of Excel. Later versions extant by the time you read this should be able to use this code.

and extend this formula down column G to the bottom of your list of prices.

This formula captures the closing price as the entry price of the position. Modify the formula to use another price if that's what you wish.

This formula displays long positions as negative values, the negative representing a cash outflow. Short positions are shown as positive values, the positive representing a cash inflow.

Next, we prepare a column which (1) computes profit or loss on the trade and (2) serves as a switch to tell the later MAE column that the trade has closed.

Assure that cells H2 and I2 are blank as row three will refer to them.

In cell H3, enter:

    =IF(G3< >G2,IF(G2>0,G2−E3,IF(G2<0,G2+E3)))

and extend the formula down to the bottom of your price list.

This formula computes the net profit or loss, exclusive of commissions and slippage, as of the close of the day when the signal in column F changes. Modify the "G2 − E3" or "G2 + E3" expressions to include commissions and/or slippage.

Finally, we compute MAE with an involved expression which (1) will not compute MAE when there is no position except on the day closing a position, (2) will not compute MAE on the opening day of the position taken at the close, (3) will compute the proper MAE on a reversal, and (4) will compute MAE using the MAX expression in Chapter 2 which compares zero, the difference between the entry and the worst price, and the previous MAE. The spreadsheet logic is tortuous but enter in cell I3:

    =IF($G3< >0,IF($G2< >0,IF($H2
    =FALSE,IF($G2<0,MAX(0,−$G2−$D3,$I2),MAX(0,$C3
      −$G2,$I2)),IF($G2<0,MAX(0,−$G2−$D3),MAX(0,$C3
      −$G2)))),IF($H3< >FALSE,IF($G2<0,MAX(0,−$G2
      −$D3,$I2),MAX(0,$C3−$G2,$I2))))

and extend the formula down to the bottom of your price range.

Here are exemplary computations for longs and shorts against which you can check your spreadsheet (Table A–1).

Long MAE Example

Table A–1 Long MAE Example. This trade goes long (indicated by a "1") on the close of 11/7/90 at 30.95. Things immediately go wrong, the low the next day reaching 30.82 for an MAE of 30.95 − 30.82 = .13. The trade ends on the close of 11/12/90. The Entry Price of −30.95 is negative to indicate a cash outflow.

Row	A	B	C	D	E	F	G	H	I
								Profit	
							Entry	or	
1	Date	Open	High	Low	Close	Position	Price	Loss	MAE
2	11/6/90	28.93	29.62	28.70	29.51				
3	11/7/90	29.40	30.95	29.30	30.95	1	−30.95	False	False
4	11/8/90	31.32	32.35	30.82	32.02	1	−30.95	False	0.13
5	11/9/90	31.50	31.97	30.42	30.59	1	−30.95	False	0.53
6	11/12/90	29.32	29.53	29.03	29.31	0	0	−1.64	1.92

Short MAE Example

Table A–2 Short MAE Example. MAE grows steadily as a short (indicated by a "−1") from 25.56 at the close of 7/12/85 goes steadily into the hole until the trade is ended on the close of 7/23/85. No MAE is computed for 7/12/85 because there is no pricing after the trade is entered on the close. On the last day of the trade, 7/23/85, adverse excursion reaches .38 as the high goes to 25.94 before the close.

Date	Open	High	Low	Close	Position	Entry Price	Profit or Loss	MAE
7/12/85	25.77	25.78	25.54	25.56	−1	25.56	False	False
7/15/85	25.43	25.66	25.37	25.59	−1	25.56	False	0.10
7/16/85	25.56	25.70	25.47	25.53	−1	25.56	False	0.14
7/17/85	25.69	25.69	25.53	25.55	−1	25.56	False	0.14
7/18/85	25.61	25.73	25.58	25.62	−1	25.56	False	0.17
7/19/85	25.58	25.62	25.52	25.57	−1	25.56	False	0.17
7/22/85	25.48	25.77	25.38	25.66	−1	25.56	False	0.21
7/23/85	25.82	25.94	25.73	25.93	0	0	−0.37	0.38

Remember, MAE never goes lower than its previous value in a trade and never goes below zero.

MIXED MAE EXAMPLE

You have an example to test your code going from long to short, here are results for a long from 5/24/89, exiting 6/9/89, shorting 6/12/89, exiting 6/23/89 in Table A–3.

Table A–3   Mixed MAE Example. Your logic should be able to handle reversals such as this and also even faster reversals shown in Figure A–4.

Date	Open	High	Low	Close	Position	Entry Price	Profit or Loss	MAE
5/24/89	17.80	18.31	17.78	18.28	1	−18.28	False	False
5/25/89	18.15	18.50	18.13	18.21	1	−18.28	False	0.15
5/26/89	18.08	18.33	18.07	18.31	1	−18.28	False	0.21
5/30/89	18.31	18.40	18.18	18.38	1	−18.28	False	0.21
5/31/89	18.36	18.42	18.22	18.27	1	−18.28	False	0.21
6/1/89	18.27	18.33	18.20	18.31	1	−18.28	False	0.21
6/2/89	18.24	18.77	18.18	18.75	1	−18.28	False	0.21
6/5/89	19.04	19.17	18.91	19.13	1	−18.28	False	0.21
6/6/89	19.08	19.12	18.81	19.11	1	−18.28	False	0.21
6/7/89	18.84	19.08	18.36	18.41	1	−18.28	False	0.21
6/8/89	18.40	18.66	18.24	18.57	1	−18.28	False	0.21
6/9/89	18.56	18.58	18.20	18.23	0	0	−0.05	0.21
6/12/89	17.93	18.01	17.58	17.61	−1	17.61	False	False
6/13/89	17.64	17.74	17.39	17.41	−1	17.61	False	0.13
6/14/89	17.66	17.73	17.22	17.57	−1	17.61	False	0.13
6/15/89	17.46	17.93	17.45	17.74	−1	17.61	False	0.32
6/16/89	17.63	17.63	17.38	17.51	−1	17.61	False	0.32
6/19/89	17.38	17.62	17.25	17.57	−1	17.61	False	0.32
6/20/89	17.58	17.74	17.52	17.58	−1	17.61	False	0.32
6/21/89	17.63	18.08	17.57	18.01	−1	17.61	False	0.47
6/22/89	18.11	18.26	17.99	18.10	−1	17.61	False	0.65
6/23/89	18.20	18.49	18.18	18.48	0	0	−0.87	0.88

MAE in Immediate Reversals

Finally, positions which go immediately from long to short (or vice versa) test your logic harshly. Table A–4 is an example the code above handled.

Table A–4 Immediate Reversal Example. Long at 21.60 on the close 10/6/92. Close and reverse on the close 10/21/92 at 21.44. Note the MAE = 21.6 − 21.37 = .23 on 10/21/92 is that for the previous long from 21.60 while the MAE = 21.48 − 21.44 = .04 on 10/22/92 is that for the short taken at the close on 10/21/92.

Date	Open	High	Low	Close	Position	Entry Price	Profit or Loss	MAE
10/6/92	21.55	21.63	21.53	21.60	1	−21.60	False	False
10/7/92	21.67	21.70	21.65	21.67	1	−21.60	False	0
10/8/92	21.71	21.78	21.70	21.73	1	−21.60	False	0
10/9/92	21.82	22.14	21.82	22.09	1	−21.60	False	0
10/12/92	22.00	22.04	21.97	22.02	1	−21.60	False	0
10/13/92	21.97	22.05	21.81	21.81	1	−21.60	False	0
10/14/92	21.81	21.89	21.77	21.81	1	−21.60	False	0
10/15/92	21.96	22.06	21.95	22.03	1	−21.60	False	0
10/16/92	22.04	22.08	21.92	21.96	1	−21.60	False	0
10/19/92	22.01	22.03	21.86	21.86	1	−21.60	False	0
10/20/92	21.83	21.92	21.79	21.83	1	−21.60	False	0
10/21/92	21.76	21.77	21.37	21.44	−1	21.44	−0.16	0.23
10/22/92	21.41	21.48	21.18	21.19	−1	21.44	False	0.04
10/23/92	21.27	21.29	21.05	21.07	−1	21.44	False	0.04
10/26/92	20.97	21.14	20.97	21.14	−1	21.44	False	0.04
10/27/92	21.23	21.24	20.93	20.94	−1	21.44	False	0.04
10/28/92	20.82	21.01	20.69	21.00	−1	21.44	False	0.04
10/29/92	20.95	20.98	20.63	20.69	−1	21.44	False	0.04
10/30/92	20.54	20.65	20.46	20.61	−1	21.44	False	0.04

I put all these computations (MAE, MaxFE, and MinFE) in the same spreadsheet, If you do this, you'll need to adjust the column references in the formulae to match your arrangement.

Appendix B

COMPUTING MAXFE

Maximum Favorable Excursion is defined and explained in Chapter 2. This appendix provides Microsoft Excel 4.0 code* which can be used as is or modified to fit your own needs.

The worksheet is structured in rows, each row representing a unit of time, usually one day.

Begin by loading Date, Open, High, Low, and Close in the first five columns, columns A, B, C, D, and E.

Next, in column F, indicate the position outstanding at the close of the day. This value is a +1 for a long position, 0 for no position, and −1 for a short position.

Any value will serve as a logical "switch" that columns to the right can use for computation. The position column can be computed or simply put in manually. If elaborate computations must be made, additional columns can be inserted before this column to handle them. In this example, the values have simply been inserted.

---

* Microsoft has been good to date about compatibility between various versions of Excel. Later versions extant by the time you read this should be able to use this code.

Next, record the price of the position taken. In cell G2 enter an initialization value of zero. In cell G3, enter

$$=IF(F2< >F3,IF(F3=1,-E3,IF(F3=-1,E3,0)),G2)$$

and extend this formula down column G to the bottom of your list of prices.

This formula captures the closing price as the entry price of the position. Modify the formula to use another price if that's what you wish.

This formula displays long positions as negative values, the negative representing a cash outflow. Short positions are shown as positive values, the positive representing a cash inflow.

Next, we prepare a column which (1) computes profit or loss on the trade and (2) serves as a switch to tell the later MaxFE column that the trade has closed.

Assure that cells H2 and I2 are blank as row three will refer to them.

In cell H3, enter:

$$=IF(G3< >G2,IF(G2>0,G2-E3,IF(G2<0,G2+E3)))$$

and extend the formula down to the bottom of your price list.

This formula computes the net profit or loss, exclusive of commissions and slippage, as of the close of the day when the signal in column F changes. Modify the "G2 − E3" or "G2 + E3" expressions to include commissions and/or slippage.

Finally, we compute MaxFE with an involved expression that (1) will not compute MaxFE when there is no position except on the day closing a position, (2) will not compute MaxFE on the opening day of the position taken at the close, (3) will compute the proper MaxFE on a reversal, and (4) will compute MaxFE using the MAX expression in Chapter 2 which compares zero, the difference between the entry and the worst price, and the previous MaxFE. The spreadsheet logic is tortuous but enter in cell I3:

=IF($G3< >0,IF($G2< >0,IF($H2
=FALSE,IF($G2<0,MAX(0,$C3+$G2,$I2),MAX(0,$G2
   −$D3,$I2)),IF($G2<0,MAX(0,$C3+$G2),MAX(0,$G3
   −$D3)))),IF($H3< >FALSE,IF(G2<0,MAX(0,C3
   +G2,I2),MAX(0,G2−D3,I2)))))

and extend the formula down to the bottom of your price range.

Here are exemplary computations for longs and shorts against which you can check your spreadsheet (Table B–1).

Table B–2 is another, more complicated example for code testing.

Table B–1 Exemplary MaxFE Computations. First long, then short but neither trade moves very far favorably. The negative −31.04 refers to the cash outflow from a long position; the positive 31.2 to the cash inflow from a short position.

	A	B	C	D	E	F	G	H	I
						Long (1) or Short			
1	Date	Open	High	Low	Close	(−1)	Entry Price	P&L	MaxFE
2	6/28/87	31.06	31.12	30.99	31.02		0		
3	6/29/87	30.95	31.08	30.87	31.04	1	−31.04	False	False
4	6/30/87	30.99	31.04	30.97	31.04	1	−31.04	False	0.00
5	7/1/87	31.15	31.21	31.15	31.19	1	−31.04	False	0.17
6	7/2/87	31.19	31.19	31.08	31.18	1	−31.04	False	0.17
7	7/6/87	31.11	31.13	31.03	31.13	0	0	0.09	0.17
8	7/7/87	30.95	31.03	30.75	31.03	0	0	False	False
9	7/8/87	31.00	31.15	30.96	31.15	0	0	False	False
10	7/9/87	31.12	31.20	31.12	31.20	−1	31.20	False	False
11	7/12/87	31.19	31.34	31.19	31.33	−1	31.20	False	0.01
12	7/13/87	31.37	31.44	31.37	31.39	−1	31.20	False	0.01
13	7/14/87	31.55	31.72	31.05	31.68	−1	31.20	False	0.15
14	7/15/87	31.66	31.70	31.57	31.67	−1	31.20	False	0.15
15	7/16/87	31.66	31.66	31.56	31.65	−1	31.20	False	0.15

Table B-2   MaxFE During Reversal. A long from 21.6 reverses to a short on the close of 10/21/92. The MaxFE for 10/21/92 is that of the long position. The MaxFE on 10/22/92 is that for the short from 21.44. The code supplied above should handle even this situation.

	A	B	C	D	E	F	G	H	I
						Long (1) or Short			
1	Date	Open	High	Low	Close	(−1)	Entry Price	P&L	MaxFE
2	10/6/92	21.55	21.63	21.53	21.60	1	−21.60	False	False
3	10/7/92	21.67	21.70	21.65	21.67	1	−21.60	False	0.10
4	10/8/92	21.71	21.78	21.7	21.73	1	−21.60	False	0.18
5	10/9/92	21.82	22.14	21.82	22.09	1	−21.60	False	0.54
6	10/12/92	22.00	22.04	21.97	22.02	1	−21.60	False	0.54
7	10/13/92	21.97	22.05	21.81	21.81	1	−21.60	False	0.54
8	10/14/92	21.81	21.89	21.77	21.81	1	−21.60	False	0.54
9	10/15/92	21.96	22.06	21.95	22.03	1	−21.60	False	0.54
10	10/16/92	22.04	22.08	21.92	21.96	1	−21.60	False	0.54
11	10/19/92	22.01	22.03	21.86	21.86	1	−21.60	False	0.54
12	10/20/92	21.83	21.92	21.79	21.83	1	−21.60	False	0.54
13	10/21/92	21.76	21.77	21.37	21.44	−1	21.44	−0.16	0.54
14	10/22/92	21.41	21.48	21.18	21.19	−1	21.44	False	0.26
15	10/23/92	21.27	21.29	21.05	21.07	−1	21.44	False	0.39
16	10/26/92	20.97	21.14	20.97	21.14	−1	21.44	False	0.47
17	10/27/92	21.23	21.24	20.93	20.94	−1	21.44	False	0.51
18	10/28/92	20.82	21.01	20.69	21.00	−1	21.44	False	0.75
19	10/29/92	20.95	20.98	20.63	20.69	−1	21.44	False	0.81
20	10/30/92	20.54	20.65	20.46	20.61	−1	21.44	False	0.98
21	11/2/92	20.72	20.76	20.55	20.70	−1	21.44	False	0.98
22	11/3/92	20.77	20.78	20.6	20.65	−1	21.44	False	0.98

Appendix C

Computing MinFE

Minimum Favorable Excursion is defined and explained in Chapter 2. This appendix provides Microsoft Excel 4.0 code* which can be used as is or modified to fit your own needs.

The worksheet is structured in rows, each row representing a unit of time, usually one day.

Begin by loading Date, Open, High, Low and Close in the first five columns, columns A, B, C, D, and E.

Next, in column F, indicate the position outstanding at the close of the day. This value is a +1 for a long position, 0 for no position, and −1 for a short position.

Any value will serve as a logical "switch" that columns to the right can use for computation. The position column can be computed or simply put in manually. If elaborate computations must be made, additional columns can be inserted before this column to handle them. In this example, the values have simply been inserted.

---

* Microsoft has been good to date about compatibility between various versions of Excel. Later versions extant by the time you read this should be able to use this code.

Next, record the price of the position taken. In cell G2 enter an initialization value of zero. In cell G3, enter

$$=IF(F2< >F3,IF(F3=1,-E3,IF(F3=-1,E3,0)),G2)$$

and extend this formula down column G to the bottom of your list of prices.

This formula captures the closing price as the entry price of the position. Modify the formula to use another price if that's what you wish.

This formula displays long positions as negative values, the negative representing a cash outflow. Short positions are shown as positive values, the positive representing a cash inflow.

Next, we prepare a column which (1) computes profit or loss on the trade and (2) serves as a switch to tell the later MinFE column that the trade has closed.

Assure that cells H2 and I2 are blank as row three will refer to them. In cell H3, enter:

$$=IF(G3< >G2,IF(G2>0,G2-E3,IF(G2<0,G2+E3)))$$

and extend the formula down to the bottom of your price list.

This formula computes the net profit or loss, exclusive of commissions and slippage, as of the close of the day when the signal in column F changes. Modify the "G2 − E3" or "G2 + E3" expressions to include commissions and/or slippage.

Finally, we compute MinFE with an involved expression that (1) will not compute MinFE when there is no position except on the day closing a position, (2) will not compute MinFE on the opening day of the position taken at the close, (3) will compute the proper MinFE on a reversal, and (4) will compute MinFE using the MAX expression in Chapter 2 which compares zero, the difference between the entry and the worst price, and the previous MinFE. The spreadsheet logic is tortuous but enter in cell I3:

=IF($G3< >0,IF($G2< >0,IF($H2
=FALSE,IF($G2<0,MAX(0,$G2+$D3,$I2),MAX(0,$G2
−C3,$I2)),IF($G2<0,MAX(0,$G2+$D3),MAX(0,$G2
−C3)))),IF($H3< >FALSE,IF($G2<0,MAX(0,$G2
+$D3,$I2),MAX(0,$G2−C3,$I2)))))

and extend the formula down to the bottom of your data range.

Here are exemplary computations for longs and shorts against which you can check your spreadsheet (Table C–1).

Table C–1 Exemplary MinFE Computations. First long (the "−21.6" refers to the cash outflow in a long position), then short, this is the most difficult situation for the spreadsheet logic to handle.

Row	A	B	C	D	E	F	G	H	I
1	Date	Open	High	Low	Close	Long (1) or Short (−1)	Entry Price	P&L	MinFE
2	10/6/92	21.55	21.63	21.53	21.60	1			
3	10/7/92	21.67	21.70	21.65	21.67	1	−21.60	False	0.05
4	10/8/92	21.71	21.78	21.70	21.73	1	−21.60	False	0.10
5	10/9/92	21.82	22.14	21.82	22.09	1	−21.60	False	0.22
6	10/12/92	22.00	22.04	21.97	22.02	1	−21.60	False	0.37
7	10/13/92	21.97	22.05	21.81	21.81	1	−21.60	False	0.37
8	10/14/92	21.81	21.89	21.77	21.81	1	−21.60	False	0.37
9	10/15/92	21.96	22.06	21.95	22.03	1	−21.60	False	0.37
10	10/16/92	22.04	22.08	21.92	21.96	1	−21.60	False	0.37
11	10/19/92	22.01	22.03	21.86	21.86	1	−21.60	False	0.37
12	10/20/92	21.83	21.92	21.79	21.83	1	−21.60	False	0.37
13	10/21/92	21.76	21.77	21.37	21.44	−1	21.44	−0.16	0.37
14	10/22/92	21.41	21.48	21.18	21.19	−1	21.44	False	0.00
15	10/23/92	21.27	21.29	21.05	21.07	−1	21.44	False	0.15
16	10/26/92	20.97	21.14	20.97	21.14	−1	21.44	False	0.30
17	10/27/92	21.23	21.24	20.93	20.94	−1	21.44	False	0.30
18	10/28/92	20.82	21.01	20.69	21.00	−1	21.44	False	0.43
19	10/29/92	20.95	20.98	20.63	20.69	−1	21.44	False	0.46
20	10/30/92	20.54	20.65	20.46	20.61	−1	21.44	False	0.79
21	11/2/92	20.72	20.76	20.55	20.70	−1	21.44	False	0.79
22	11/3/92	20.77	20.78	20.60	20.65	−1	21.44	False	0.79
23	11/4/92	20.40	20.44	20.28	20.40	−1	21.44	False	1.00

Appendix D

GENERATING A FREQUENCY DISTRIBUTION

Instructions for setting up a frequency distribution will vary by the software you're using. These are generic instructions for Microsoft Excel. It's important to master this technique because, otherwise, generating the graphs shown in this book is extremely tedious.

For this example, a spreadsheet was prepared as in Appendix A and two new columns, J and K, were added. The rows, as before, are each day's prices and computations. Therefore, the columns are as follows:

A	Date
B	Open
C	High
D	Low
E	Close
F	Position (Long +1, Short −1)
G	Entry Price
H	Profit or loss on the trade at close
I	MAE
J	Winning MAE
K	Losing MAE

To prepare column J, go to cell J3, enter:

$$=IF(H3<>FALSE,IF(H3>0,I3))$$

and extend the formula down to the end of your data array. In column K, go to K3, enter

$$=IF(H3<>FALSE,IF(H3<0,I3))$$

and extend the formula down to the last line of your data. These two formula record the MAE if it's a winner or loser, respectively. Otherwise, they enter a FALSE value which won't be picked up by the function creating the frequency distribution.

Now, go to the last line of your data array. The spreadsheet I used for this book has 3,069 lines or rows, so all the formulae were extended to row 3069. Just below the last line, in cell J3070 (or the equivalent in your spreadsheet) enter:

$$= count(j3:j3069)$$

In cell K3070, enter:

$$= count(i3:i3069)$$

These two counts will serve as checksums on the frequency distribution. This is a good place to enter other statistical measures such as average, median, skew, and kurtosis. If you know what these are, you'll know how to put them in! For the graphically oriented amongst us, let's get on with making the graph. Make these entries:

Cell I3070	MAE
Cell J3070	Winners
Cell K3070	Losers

Next we make the categories by telling the spreadsheet the size of each bin. Enter:

Cell I3071   .15

In cell I3072 enter:

$$= I3071 + .15$$

and extend that cell's formula from I3072 down to cell I3084 which should produce a value of 2.1 in cell I3084. You should now have something that looks like this:

	I	J	K
3070	MAE	Winners	Losers
3071	0.15		
3072	0.30		
3073	0.45		
3074	0.60		
3075	0.75		
3076	0.90		
3077	1.05		
3078	1.20		
3079	1.35		
3080	1.50		
3081	1.65		
3082	1.80		
3083	1.95		
3084	2.10		

To make the distributions, select cells J3071 through J3085* and type (Don't ENTER!):

$$= frequency(j3:j3069,I3071:I3084)$$

Then, if you're brightly using a Mac, while holding down the ⌘ key, press ENTER. If you're using a Windows machine, press CTRL + SHIFT + ENTER for the same result.

---

* You select through J3085 to allow a cell for overflow if the bins you specify don't allow for the full range of occurrences.

To make the distribution for losing MAE, select cells K3071 through K3085 and type:

$$= frequency(j3{:}j3069, I3071{:}I3084)$$

before pressing ⌘ + ENTER or CTRL + SHIFT + ENTER as your machine dictates. You know have the raw distributions to which I have added checksums at the bottom:

	I	J	K
3070	MAE	Winners	Losers
3071	0.15	80	21
3072	0.30	17	44
3073	0.45	4	28
3074	0.60	0	28
3075	0.75	0	7
3076	0.90	1	10
3077	1.05	1	2
3078	1.20	0	3
3079	1.35	0	1
3080	1.50	1	0
3081	1.65	0	0
3082	1.80	0	1
3083	1.95	0	2
3084	2.10	0	1
3085		0	0
3086		104	148

Finally, to get to the graphics, highlight I3070 through K3084 and step through the graphic routine for your spreadsheet. For Excel 4.0 for the Mac, select ⌘ + N, then C, then return. That will give you the basic graph which you can then customize as you like.

Appendix **E**

MAE for
Shorts and Longs

You would like to distinguish between the MAE distributions for short positions and that for long positions, probably because you feel the adverse price movement in those two situations is different. If it were different, you'd adjust your stops and reverse point differently depending on the direction of your trade. This appendix shows you some Excel code that you can use to construct the two charts you'll need to analyze this.

To begin with, lay out the data as described in Appendix D, to wit:

Column	Information in Column
A	Date
B	Open
C	High
D	Low
E	Close
F	Position (Long +1, Short −1)
G	Entry Price
H	Profit or loss on the trade at close
I	MAE

Use the same entries described in those Appendices to fill in the data. (An example is below). Then, label column J as "Short MAE" and in cell J3 enter:

Short MAE	Long MAE
=IF(G3<0,I3)	=IF(G3>0,I3)

These two columns will extract from the MAE column, column I, the MAE values if the position is long or short and it will extract them on a daily basis. Extend the formulae in row 3 down to the bottom of your data range.

Next create four new columns as follows:

Winning Long MAE	Losing Long MAE	Winning Short MAE	Long Short MAE
=IF($H3< > FALSE,IF($G2 <0,IF($H3> 0,$I3)))	=IF($H3< > FALSE,IF($G2 <0,IF($H3< 0,$I3)))	=IF($H3< > FALSE,IF($G2 >0,IF($H3> 0,$I3)))	=IF($H3< > FALSE,IF($G2 >0,IF($H3< 0,$I3)))

These formulae will check (1) if a position has closed, (2) if it was a long or a short (by looking in column G), and (3) if it was a winner or a loser. The column with the formula that checks out will transfer the MAE value into itself; otherwise, it will set the cell to FALSE, a reading which is ignored by the summary statistical functions we'll use next. Table E–1 is an exemplary table against which you can check your code.

Next, you summarize the data in columns L through O just as it was summarized in Appendix D. In cells L22 through O22 enter the labels for the graph you're creating:

Row	L	M	N	O
22	Winners, Long	Losers, Long	Winners, Short	Losers, Short

In cells, K23 through K33 enter the sizes of the bins you want. In this example, I've arbitrarily set the bin size to .1. You can enter any

Table E-1   Long/Short MAE Computation. This table of artificial prices shows all four possible combinations of winning and losing while being long or short. The code described in this appendix generates either a FALSE or the MAE value for the correct situation in columns L, M, N, and O.

Row	A	B	C	D	E	F	G	H	I	J	K
						Long (1) or Short	Entry			Short	Long
1	Date	Open	High	Low	Close	(−1)	Price	P&L	MAE	MAE	MAE
2	6/28/87	31.06	31.12	30.99	31.02		0				
3	6/29/87	30.95	31.08	30.87	31.04	1	−31.04	False	False	False	False
4	6/30/87	30.99	31.04	30.97	31.04	1	−31.04	False	0.07	0.07	False
5	7/1/87	31.15	31.21	31.15	31.19	1	−31.04	False	0.07	0.07	False
6	7/2/87	31.19	31.19	31.08	31.18	1	−31.04	False	0.07	0.07	False
7	7/6/87	31.11	31.13	31.03	31.13	0	0	0.09	0.07	False	False
8	7/7/87	30.95	31.03	30.75	31.03	0	0	False	False	False	False
9	7/8/87	31.00	31.15	30.96	31.15	0	0	False	False	False	False
10	7/9/87	31.12	31.20	31.12	31.20	−1	31.20	False	False	False	False
11	7/12/87	31.05	31.30	31.05	31.14	−1	31.20	False	0.10	False	0
12	7/13/87	31.13	31.31	30.85	30.90	−1	31.20	False	0.11	False	0.1
13	7/14/87	30.95	31.01	30.60	30.60	−1	31.20	False	0.11	False	0.1
14	7/15/87	30.54	30.58	30.32	30.40	0	0	0.8	0.11	False	False
15	7/16/87	30.40	30.42	30.38	30.40	1	−30.40	False	False	False	False
16	7/19/87	30.24	30.30	30.20	30.20	1	−30.40	False	0.20	0.20	False
17	7/20/87	30.20	30.23	30.18	30.18	1	−30.40	False	0.22	0.22	False
18	7/21/87	30.14	30.15	30.05	30.10	0	0	−0.3	0.35	False	False
19	7/22/87	30.10	30.12	30.10	30.12	−1	30.12	False	False	False	False
20	7/23/87	30.20	30.48	30.19	30.45	−1	30.12	False	0.36	False	0.3
21	7/26/87	30.50	30.55	30.48	30.54	0	0	−0.4	0.43	False	False

value you wish and you can have more bins or fewer bins as you think necessary. Here you end up with values from .1 to 1.0.

Select the range from L23 to L34 and type—but don't hit ENTER—

$$= \text{frequency } (13:121,k23:k33)$$

and, while holding down the ♥ key, press ENTER. If you're using a Windows machine, press CTRL + SHIFT + ENTER for the same result. The entire range is filled automatically by EXCEL; you don't need to extend the formula down. Normally, you'd have far more rows than just three through twenty-one, so you'd adjust "13:21" in the formula to match the range you want checked. If your range of bins were more or less than "K23:K33" you'd adjust that as well.

Just so you can be sure, you follow the same procedure for columns M, N, and O. Each time, select the range from row 23 to row 34. Here are the formulae for each column:

M	N	O
= FREQUENCY (M3:M21,K23:K33)	= FREQUENCY (N3:N21,K23:K33)	= FREQUENCY (O3:O21,K23:K33)

After adding cells summing the distributions at the bottom of the table, you should end up with something like this:

Table E–2 Frequency Distributions. The distribution of adverse excursions from the sample table in Table E–1 is very small, there being only one example of each case.

Row	K	L	M	N	O
22		Winners, Long	Losers, Long	Winners, Short	Losers, Short
23	0.1	1	0	0	0
24	0.2	0	0	1	0
25	0.3	0	0	0	0
26	0.3	0	0	0	0
27	0.4	0	1	0	0
28	0.5	0	0	0	1
29	0.6	0	0	0	0
30	0.7	0	0	0	0
31	0.8	0	0	0	0
32	0.9	0	0	0	0
33	1.0	0	0	0	0
34	Overflow	0	0	0	0
35	Totals	1	1	1	1

It would do no good to draw a chart of this example since there is only one of each case. I leave it to you to draw one chart of K22:M33 and another chart of K22:K33,N22:O33. You'd the compare the stop points you'd pick off each chart to see if there were a material difference.

Appendix F

COMPUTING PROFIT CURVES

COMPUTATION

It isn't always possible to pick out a stop and/or reverse point just from a frequency diagram. That only shows the number of trades that have taken place in each MAE bin and, frequently, the curve for winners will overlap the curve for losers. To sort this out, using the same bins, compute the profit or loss from the winners and losers and plot the two curves for comparison. Chapter 4 outlines this process generally with tables. This appendix shows you some Excel code that you can use to construct the charts you'll need to analyze this.

To begin with, lay out the data as described in previous appendices as follows:

Column	Information in Column
A	Date
B	Open
C	High
D	Low
E	Close
F	Position (Long +1, Short −1)
G	Entry Price
H	Profit or loss on the trade at close
I	MAE
J	Winning MAE
K	Losing MAE
L	MinFE*
M	MaxFE

* For exposition, MinFE and MaxFE were shown in column I. Now move them to columns L and M by rearranging columns.

See columns A through I of Table E–1. You should have something like this:

A	B	C	D	E	F	G	H	I	J	K
					Long (1) or Short (−1)	Entry Price			Winning	Losing
Date	Open	High	Low	Close			P&L	MAE	MAE	MAE
6/28/87	31.06	31.12	30.99	31.02		0				
6/29/87	30.95	31.08	30.87	31.04	1	−31.04	False	False	False	False
6/30/87	30.99	31.04	30.97	31.04	1	−31.04	False	0.07	False	False
7/1/87	31.15	31.21	31.15	31.19	1	−31.04	False	0.07	False	False
7/2/87	31.19	31.19	31.08	31.18	1	−31.04	False	0.07	False	False
7/6/87	31.11	31.13	31.03	31.13	0	0	0.09	0.07	0.07	False
7/7/87	30.95	31.03	30.75	31.03	0	0	False	False	False	False
7/8/87	31.00	31.15	30.96	31.15	0	0	False	False	False	False
7/9/87	31.12	31.20	31.12	31.20	−1	31.20	False	False	False	False
7/12/87	31.05	31.30	31.05	31.14	−1	31.20	False	0.10	False	False
7/13/87	31.13	31.31	30.85	30.90	−1	31.20	False	0.11	False	False
7/14/87	30.95	31.01	30.60	30.60	−1	31.20	False	0.11	False	False
7/15/87	30.54	30.58	30.32	30.40	0	0	0.8	0.11	0.11	False
7/16/87	30.40	30.42	30.38	30.40	1	−30.40	False	False	False	False
7/19/87	30.24	30.30	30.20	30.20	1	−30.40	False	0.20	False	False
7/20/87	30.20	30.23	30.18	30.18	1	−30.40	False	0.22	False	False
7/21/87	30.14	30.15	30.05	30.10	0	0	−0.3	0.35	False	0.35
7/22/87	30.10	30.12	30.10	30.12	−1	30.12	False	False	False	False
7/23/87	30.20	30.48	30.19	30.45	−1	30.12	False	0.36	False	False
7/26/87	30.50	30.55	30.48	30.54	0	0	−0.4	0.43	False	0.43

The table to be created here will have the MAE bins' values across the top of the columns. I set them for this example at .11, .21, .31, .41, .51, and .61 which values will vary as you change the size of the bins during your analysis. These would be your stops. The .11 stop would allow adverse excursion up to .10 before being triggered, for example.

The rows will be each day (or week, month or period). The result in each cell of the table will be the end-of-the-day **closed** equity from all the trades to date, assuming the trades were stopped at .01 less than the column heading (that is, stopped at .1 for the first column, .2 for the second column and so on).

First put in the column headings as:

Row	N	O	P	Q	R	S
1	0.11	0.21	0.31	0.41	0.51	0.61

Then, in cell N3, enter:

$$=IF(\$H3<>FALSE,IF(N\$1<$$
$$=ROUND(\$I3,2),N2-N\$1,N2+\$H3),N2)$$

and extend this formula to the right to, in this example, cell S3. Then extend N3 through S3 (in Excel notation N3:S3) down to the bottom of your data range. The results for columns N through S are shown in Table F-1.

To be sure you understand the calculations, you should work through the impact of each of the four trades here. This will be important later when you analyze changing stops and wonder why the results aren't always intuitive.

The first trade closes on row 7 with an adverse excursion of just .07. None of the stops are tripped and the profit booked to date is increased by the trades profit of .09. This is the simplest case possible.

Next, in row 14, a trade closes with a profit of .8 (80 ticks) and an MAE of .11. Looking at cell N14, you can see the impact of tripping the stop set at .11. Instead of adding 80 points of profit as in cell O14, eleven points of loss is added from the stop's being executed: .09 − .11 = −.02.

Table F-1 Profit Curves. Too tight a stop at .11 causes losses in this sample data while looser stops are profitable. Row 21 will be the summary-to-date of each stop's impact.

Row	N	O	P	Q	R	S
1	0.11	0.21	0.31	0.41	0.51	0.61
2						
3	0.00	0.00	0.00	0.00	0.00	0.00
4	0.00	0.00	0.00	0.00	0.00	0.00
5	0.00	0.00	0.00	0.00	0.00	0.00
6	0.00	0.00	0.00	0.00	0.00	0.00
7	0.09	0.09	0.09	0.09	0.09	0.09
8	0.09	0.09	0.09	0.09	0.09	0.09
9	0.09	0.09	0.09	0.09	0.09	0.09
10	0.09	0.09	0.09	0.09	0.09	0.09
11	0.09	0.09	0.09	0.09	0.09	0.09
12	0.09	0.09	0.09	0.09	0.09	0.09
13	0.09	0.09	0.09	0.09	0.09	0.09
14	−0.02	0.89	0.89	0.89	0.89	0.89
15	−0.02	0.89	0.89	0.89	0.89	0.89
16	−0.02	0.89	0.89	0.89	0.89	0.89
17	−0.02	0.89	0.89	0.89	0.89	0.89
18	−0.13	0.68	0.58	0.59	0.59	0.59
19	−0.13	0.68	0.58	0.59	0.59	0.59
20	−0.13	0.68	0.58	0.59	0.59	0.59
21	−0.24	0.47	0.27	0.18	0.17	0.17

In cell N18, a trade with a loss of .3 and an MAE of .35 causes the stop at .11 to be tripped limiting the loss. The cell is changed as $-.02 - .11 = -.13$ instead of losing 30 ticks (.3). Cell O18 is calculated as $.89 - .21 = .68$ from the stop set at .21. In Cell P18, the stop at .31 generates this calculation: $.89 - .31 = .58$. In Cell Q18, the stop is not tripped and the loss is just .3, so the cell is calculated as $.89 - .3 = .59$.

Row 21 is the last trade shown with a loss of .4 and an MAE of .43. I leave it to you to verify the computations of the cell's values.

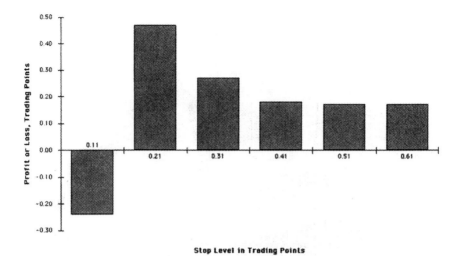

Figure F–1 Profit vs. Stop Level. A tight stop at .11 produces losses while profits peak with a stop of .21 using the sample data in this Appendix. Results aren't always so neat but the display is typical.

GRAPHIC DISPLAY

To display the data graphically, select N1:S1 and N21:S21.* Then order up a chart of the selected range.† Figure F–1 is the result using the numbers in Table F–1.

In Figure F–1, N1:S1 are the stop levels specified in the worksheet, all set one tick higher than the limits of the bins used for analysis.

Interpreting Figure F–1 is straightforward since all we seek is a point for placing a stop. This (limited) experience shows that a stop at .21 would generate the most profit.

Occasionally, you'll have two or three stop levels that are close to each other in profitability at the end of a long run of trades. It may be

---

* See your spreadsheet's manual for non-contiguous selection. In Excel 4.0, hold down the key when selecting additional ranges of cells.

† In Excel 4.0, type N, C, return. In Excel 5.0, select the Chart Wizard button and follow instructions.

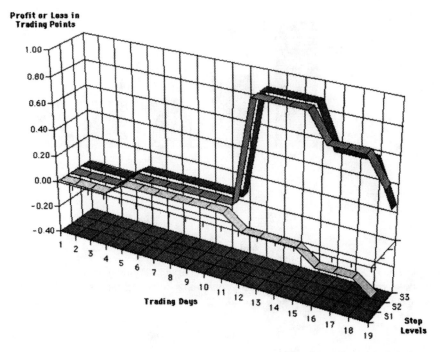

Figure F–2   Closed Profit or Loss Over Time. Using the three dimensional chart-ing capability in a spreadsheet, the numbers in Table F–1 generate information about which stop levels perform best over the trading period.

that one performed better prior to the end of trading and you'd like to check that. You can plot the equity performance of all three stop lev-els over time using the 3D graphics functions in your spreadsheet. Using Table F–1 as the example, select N3:P21, generate a chart and, if it's not your default option, change the display to a three dimen-sional line drawing.*

Figure F–2 with its four trades doesn't tell you much more than the ending results of Figure F–1 but it does show that the lowest stop generates the slowest rate of decline when the two-trade losing streak hits toward the end of trading. This sort of inspection of a long series of trades may be valuable to a trader picking stops for the future.

---

* Excel users can consult the Gallery in Excel 4.0 and the Chart Wizard in Excel 5.0.

Appendix G

RANGE AND VOLATILITY

Here are some examples from a variety of tradables showing the relationship of range to volatility. These graphs may give you some trading ideas for tracking volatility using range as a proxy or for adjusting entry points on volatility-based trading systems. Naturally, this book is concerned with the effects expanded ranges have on stops.

Each graph (Figures G–1 through G–4) has been prepared using a standard computation of volatility for twenty days (to pick a number). From the high-low range for each day, the moving, twenty-day, simple average was computed. The two series were mean-normalized by adjusting the volatility's mean to that of the range's, giving a graphic where the coincident fluctuations of both were highlighted.

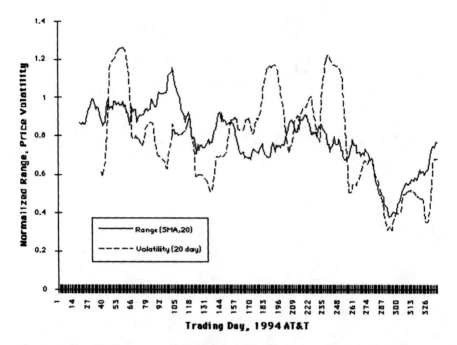

Figure G–1 AT&T Range and Volatility. Though not consistent in their fluctuation, changes in range and volatility in AT&T during early 1995 often coincided but occasionally diverged over longer periods.

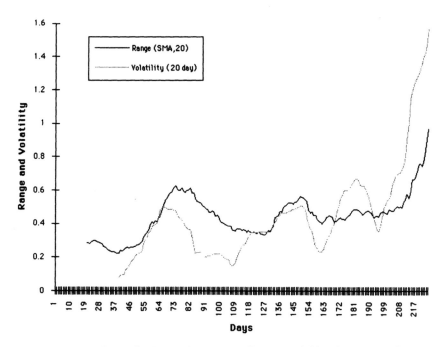

Figure G–2 Coffee Volatility and Range. Coffee, a tradable of immense fluctuations shows that while range can change as volatility changes, it can remain at higher levels even as volatility recedes.

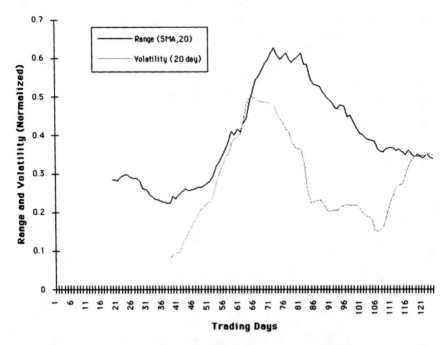

Figure G–3   June 1995 U.S. Treasury Bond Futures. Leads and lags in the changes of range and volatility are apparent in this graph of the futures contract's activity. Though only a short extract of time, it suggests that range expansion or contraction may precede volatility expansion or contraction, a neat intuitive result.

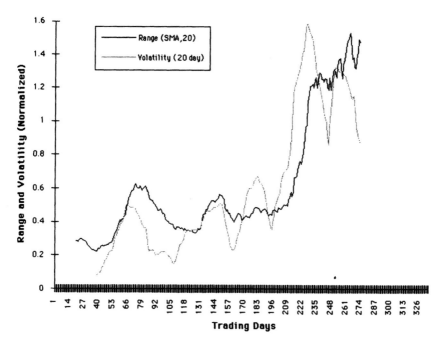

Figure G–4   Dow Industrials' Range and Volatility. While daily range (smoothed) certainly fluctuates, the associated volatility moves much more quickly to produce sharper peaks and valleys than that of the smoothed range. The coincidence of these two lines suggests the range/volatility relationship may be most applicable in indices where the law of large numbers has great effect.

Appendix H

RANGE EXCURSION

This appendix shows how you'd check to see if range expands or contracts after your combination of tradable and trading rules calls for a trade. This programs an exemplary spreadsheet to demonstrate one way of approaching the question.

To begin with, lay out the data as described in previous appendices in Table H–1. Notice that I've kept columns I through M for MinFE and MaxFE, respectively, but in the tabular output below, I've suppressed their printing to save space here.

Devote the first 63 rows to data so that the trading system has all the data needs on row 64. Then go to cell N60 and, beginning from there, enter column headings as below in Figure H–1.

Table H-1 Spreadsheet Setup. To be consonant with previous appendices, extend the spreadsheet you've already got rightward by adding columns for the range computations.

Column	Information in Column
A	Date
B	Open
C	High
D	Low
E	Close
F	Position (Long +1, Short −1)
G	Entry Price
H	Profit or loss on the trade at close
I	MAE
J	Winning MAE
K	Losing MAE
L	MinFE*
M	MaxFE

* For exposition, MinFE and MaxFE were shown in column I. Now move them to columns L and M by rearranging columns.

After the headings are all entered, begin in Cell N 64 and make the following entries, leaving cell T64 blank:

Cell	Cell Entry
N64	=ROUND((SUM(C45:C64)−SUM(D45:D64))/20,2)
O64	=C64−D64
P64	=IF(G64< >0,O64−N64)
Q64	=IF(G64< >0,IF(G64< >G63,0,MAX(Q63,C64−D64)))
R64	=IF(G64< >0,Q64−N64)
S64	=IF($G64< >0,IF($F64< >$F63,$N64))
U64	=IF(G64< >0,O64−T64)

	H	O	P	Q	R	S	T	U
60								Over &
61	Daily		Over or				Range at	Under
62	Range	Day's	Under	Max	Range	Range at	Entry, Life	Range at
63	SMA20	Range	SMA20	Range	Expansion	Entry	of Trade	Entry

Figure H–1   Column Headings. To prepare for the computation of range expansion, enter these headings in these cells. If you prefer to put headings on the top row, that's fine, too. Formula entry will start on cell N64. ("SMA20" is a mnemonic for 20-day simple moving average.)

Next select N64:U65 and hit CMD-D to extend the formulas down one line. Then go to cell T64 and enter:

Cell	Cell Entry
T65	=IF($G65< >0,IF($F65< >$F64,$N65,T64))

Lastly, you extend to the bottom of your data rows. If that data ended on row 300, for example, select N65:U300* and hit CMD-D. Excel may give you a warning that it cannot proceed unless there is no Undo. If so, accept the warning and proceed anyway. This should extend all formulas down to the bottom of your model creating the data series for your inspection.

GRAPHICS

Because different versions of Excel have differing interfaces to specify graphics I'll restrict myself to getting the data into place for graphing as shown in the text.

The values computed above create strings of values during the trades. Since there is no way to know where in the column they will

---

* You can select large areas like this without clicking and dragging by going to the upper leftmost cell, selecting Go To (with a CMD—G or from a menu) entering the bottom rightmost cell's number, and hitting SHIFT-RETURN.

occur and you should graph each from the day the trade starts you must tediously cut these strings, transpose and especially paste them into a second worksheet where their statistical properties and graphics can be processed.

Therefore create two new worksheets, one for comparing ranges after entry to a running 20-day simple moving average and a second for comparing those ranges to the range exactly at entry. Take extra precautions to keep these two spreadsheets separate.

Each spreadsheet will have two blocks of data. The first block will be, roughly from A3:AZ36 and the second from, roughly, A38:AZ65. These can be changed as you need. The number of rows is dependent on the number of trades and the number of columns is dependent on how many days the trades go on. If you don't want to transpose the values from vertical, as they are in the model above to horizontal, these two blocks should be arranged vertically rather than horizontally.

Begin with the headlines, examples of which are in Figure H–2 which shows the beginning of the block for Winners. I put the title for Losers in cell B38. As an example, I use the comparison of range to the moving 20-day average of range.

Once the headlines are set, return to the original model first constructed in this appendix (I'll refer to it as the range expansion model). Go to your first trade which, for example, looks like Table H–2.

Next switch over to the Graphics Worksheet and select cell A5. From the menu, select EDIT Paste Special. In the pop up window, select Paste Values and click the box for Transpose, then click OK (or hit Return). The values themselves will be laid out as shown in Figure H–2.

Next, return to the range expansion model and go to your next trade by proceeding down the column. As before, highlight the entire series of values, copy the series, return to the graphics worksheet, and

	A	B	C	D	E	F	G	H
1		This worksheet compares the 20-day average range each day to the range on each day of the trade.						
2		Remember to chop off the first day because that range was BEFORE the entry at the close.						
3		Winners						
4								
5	-0.11	-0.12	-0.07					

Figure H–2 Titles for Graphics Worksheet. Take care to keep the worksheets for the two different range expansion measures separate with embedded comments. Data for the first trade begins on row five.

Table H–2 Selecting Values to Transpose. The bordered values should be highlighted (selected) and copied.

Daily Range SMA20	Day's Range	Over or Under SMA20	Max Range	Range Expansion	Range at Entry	Range at Entry, Life of Trade	Over and Under Range at Entry
0.18	0.07	−0.11	0.07	−0.11	False		0.07
0.18	0.06	−0.12	0.07	−0.11	False	0	0.06
0.18	0.11	−0.07	0.11	−0.07	False	0	0.11
0.18	0.10	False	False	False	False	False	False
0.18	0.28	False	False	False	False	False	False
0.19	0.19	False	False	False	False	False	False
0.19	0.08	−0.11	0	−0.19	0.19	0.19	−0.11
0.19	0.15	−0.04	0.15	−0.04	False	0.19	−0.04

paste them specially, if the trade is a winner, into cell A6. If it is a loser, paste it into cell A39. Continue this until all the measured range expansions for the approach of comparing to the 20-day average have been transposed into the graphics worksheet. Use the same procedure for comparing range expansions to the price at entry but use the other graphics worksheet to paste your values.

To create the analytical graphics in Chapter 5 use the following approaches. For the daily range excursions such as Figure 5–4 select the full range of winning cells, create a chart and change the chart type to XY (Scatter). You can select either just winners, just losers, or both. (Use the command key while highlighting to select non-contiguous data points.) For line charts like Figures 5–5 to 5–6, change the chart type to line.

I put the statistical summary functions at the bottom of each worksheet. To create Figure 5–7, I installed frequency distributions in cells A77:A91. These are a little tricky to enter so let me describe it practically. In cell B77, put the title "Losers" and in C77 put "Winners." Then, in cells A78:A90, put −.7, −.5, −.3, −.1, 0, .1, .3, .5, .7, .9, 1.1, 1.3, and 1.5. Next select cells B78:B91 (yes, that's 91) and type in the following:

= FREQUENCY(B39:AV65,A78:A90)

	A	B	C
77		Losers	Winners
78	-0.7	=FREQUENCY(B39:AV65,A78:A90)	=FREQUENCY(B5:AV35,A78:A90)
79	-0.5	=FREQUENCY(B39:AV65,A78:A90)	=FREQUENCY(B5:AV35,A78:A90)
80	-0.3	=FREQUENCY(B39:AV65,A78:A90)	=FREQUENCY(B5:AV35,A78:A90)
81	-0.1	=FREQUENCY(B39:AV65,A78:A90)	=FREQUENCY(B5:AV35,A78:A90)
82	0	=FREQUENCY(B39:AV65,A78:A90)	=FREQUENCY(B5:AV35,A78:A90)
83	0.1	=FREQUENCY(B39:AV65,A78:A90)	=FREQUENCY(B5:AV35,A78:A90)
84	0.3	=FREQUENCY(B39:AV65,A78:A90)	=FREQUENCY(B5:AV35,A78:A90)
85	0.5	=FREQUENCY(B39:AV65,A78:A90)	=FREQUENCY(B5:AV35,A78:A90)
86	0.7	=FREQUENCY(B39:AV65,A78:A90)	=FREQUENCY(B5:AV35,A78:A90)
87	0.9	=FREQUENCY(B39:AV65,A78:A90)	=FREQUENCY(B5:AV35,A78:A90)
88	1.1	=FREQUENCY(B39:AV65,A78:A90)	=FREQUENCY(B5:AV35,A78:A90)
89	1.3	=FREQUENCY(B39:AV65,A78:A90)	=FREQUENCY(B5:AV35,A78:A90)
90	1.5	=FREQUENCY(B39:AV65,A78:A90)	=FREQUENCY(B5:AV35,A78:A90)
91		=FREQUENCY(B39:AV65,A78:A90)	=FREQUENCY(B5:AV35,A78:A90)
92		=SUM(B78:B91)	=SUM(C78:C91)

Figure H–3 Frequency Distribution Expressions. These formulations summarize the distribution of winners and losers' range expansions in the graphics worksheet.

BUT, don't hit the return key. Instead, hold down the command button and hit the enter key. This will extend the frequency distribution, using the categories in A78:A90 throughout the range and put any overflow into cell B91. Note that this is sorting all the data points in the range B39:AV65, the range where all the losering trades range expansions lie.

	A	B	C
67		Losers	Winners
68	n (number of days in trades)	=COUNT(B39:AV65)	=COUNT(B5:AV35)
69	Max	=MAX(B39:AV65)	=MAX(B5:AV35)
70	Min	=MIN(B39:AV65)	=MIN(B5:AV35)
71	Average	=AVERAGE(B39:AV65)	=AVERAGE(B5:AV35)
72	Std. Deviation	=STDEV(B39:AV65)	=STDEV(B5:AV35)
73	Skew	=SKEW(B39:AV65)	=SKEW(B5:AV35)
74	Kurtosis	=KURT(B39:AV65)	=KURT(B5:AV35)

Figure H–4 Summary Statistics for Range Expansion. These formulas can be used to generate the usual parametric stats for range expansion. (See Table 5–1.) Since most of the value of range analysis comes via inspection, these are usually good for spotlighting errors when they come up with some unusual values.

For the winners highlight C78:C91 and enter

$$= FREQUENCY(B5:AV35,A78:A90)$$

Your result should look like Figure H–3 if you turn Excel's display options to Display Formulas.

From this point on, graphics are a snap. Select A77:C90, summon a chart, change the chart type to column, and customize it to your content.

I also put in a summary statistics section in these worksheet at Cell A67. Figure H–4 shows the formulas used.

Appendix I

MARTINGALES

This appendix gives the instructions for creating martingale models in Excel. Begin with a blank spreadsheet, laying out the headings like Figure I–1.

The first eight rows are shown here but only the first four involve headings. The computations beginning in row 5 will be taken up in a minute.

Row 1 entries are text titles. Put them in the indicated columns. In Row two, insert the value .5 in C2, 1.0 in D2 and $310 in F2. Complete the headings by typing in the text for row 4 in each indicated column. "Bet Table" is in cell G4.

	A	B	C	D	E	F	G	H
1	Assumptions:		P(WIN)	Win / $ Loss		Bet Size		
2			0.5	1		$310		
3								
4	Trade	Bet	Win or Loss	Contracts Loss/Gain	Equity Units	$ Equity	Bet Table	
5	1	1	LOSS	-1	-1	($310)	-45	10
6	2	2	WIN	2	1	$310	-36	9
7	3	0	FALSE	0	1	$310	-28	8
8	4	0	FALSE	0	1	$310	-27	8

Figure I–1 Headings Layout. This screen capture shows the model's headings. Rows one through four are text or fixed values used in the calculations below.

The probability of a win can be varied later in the model; it's set to .5 here for convenience and because the resulting calculations don't get out of hand. The value in D2, set to 1, is actually the ratio of the average win (in dollars) to the average loss in dollars. This allows you to adjust this crucial factor land see the impact on your equity and loss drawdowns immediately. Last, F2 is set to $310, the MAE and average loss for the Crude data used in this book. This is a little harsh; some trades could be losers without hitting the MAE stop. The model itself deals mostly with trading units but this allows a convenient calculation of dollar impacts. You could make it worse by adding in slippage and commissions.

COMPUTATIONS

To enter the computations, row 5 is given the initial values where needed and row 6 is given the formulations. Then, row 6 is just extended downward to row 24 by highlighting A5:F24. NOTICE that the Bet Table in columns G and H is entered manually. It's values are not formulas but specific values that Excel will look up depending on the state of the equity units in column E. I've created this table from a complex martingale so that you can quickly look up your "bet" without going through the martingale logic. The martingale used is a slightly modified version of that published by Bob Pelletier.*

Enter these values in row 5:

Column/Row	Value or Expression
A5	1
B5	1
C5	=IF(B5=0,FALSE,IF(RAND()>C$2,"LOSS","WIN"))
D5	= IF(C5="LOSS",−B5,B5*D$2)
E5	=D5
F5	=E5*F$2

---

* Pelletier, Robert C. "Martingale Money Management" Stocks and Commodities, V. 7.3 (Seattle, 1988) pp. 69–72 and "Money Management for Martingale Commodity Traders" *The Journal of Commodity Trading,* 4(3).

Before entering expressions in rows six and below, build the lookup table so you won't get any error messages when you enter your formulas. The lookup table contains the bet size for most of the equity balances you'll run into, though not all. The model's capacity can be exceeded with long, involved runs of wins and losses, in which case you'll get an "N/A" error. Ignore it and recalculate. This simplification is preferable to the involved logic you'd type in to get Excel to fully simulate a complex martingale.

Enter this table manually beginning with "Bet Table" in cell G4.

	Bet Table	
Row	**G**	**H**
5	−45	10
6	−36	9
7	−28	8
8	−27	8
9	−21	7
10	−20	10
11	−19	8
12	−15	6
13	−14	6
14	−11	8
15	−10	5
16	−9	5
17	−8	6
18	−6	4
19	−5	4
20	−4	5
21	−3	3
22	−2	3
23	−1	2
24	0	1

To activate this table, the range it covers needs to be named. Highlight G5:H24 and select Formula/Define Name.* In the dialogue

---

* Excel versions differ somewhat in defining names. Check your documentation to get the specifics for your version.

that comes up, give the range the name "Bet_Table" using the lower
dash (SHIFT-Dash), not the normal dash on the upper right of your
keyboard. Click OK to close the popup window.

Next enter these values in row 6:

Column/Row	Value or Expression
A6=	A5+1
B6=	IF(E5>0,0VLOOKUP(E5,Bet_Table,2))

The value in B6 will use the lookup table just entered.

Now highlight C5:F24 and hit CMD-D. This should extend the
formulas down to row 24. Similarly, highlight A6:B24 and hit CMD-
D again. Your model should now look like Table I–1, although the values in the cells will be different.

EXPLANATIONS

Column A is a simple counter, for convenience only. Note that the
counter numbers and the model's row numbers do NOT match.

Column B computes the bet size using the Bet Table which consists of all the values from G5 to H24. When a cell in Column B sees
that the Equity Units in Column E after the previous trade are zero
or negative, it looks through Column G of the Bet Table for the value
it sees in the Equity Units column. Then it picks the value adjacent to
that value in Column H. For example, trade 2 sees a −1 in the Equity
Units column. Going to the Bet Table, it finds −1 near the bottom and
brings back the value of 2 that it sees in the adjacent column. Thus,
trade number 2 bets 2 contracts or blocks of shares.

Column C computes a random value between 0 and .9999. It compares that to the hurdle for winning set in cell C2 and decides whether
the trade is to be a win or a loss.

Column D takes the win/loss decision and computes the number
of units won or lost. If it's a loss, it's just the number of units bet. If
it's a win, its the number of units times the ratio of win size to loss
size specified in cell D2.

Table I-1 Completed Martingale Model. Endure eighteen trades to win $310 while tying up $4,340 plus margin. Experiences like that minimize the appeal of Martingales but at least they generally come out to the good.

Assumptions:		P(WIN) 0.5	$ Win / $ Loss 1		Bet Size $310		
		Win or	Contracts	Equity			
Trade	Bet	Loss	Loss/Gain	Units	Equity	Bet	Table
1	1	Loss	−1	−1	$(310)	−45	10
2	2	Win	2	1	310	−36	9
3	0	False	0	1	310	−28	8
4	0	False	0	1	310	−27	8
5	0	False	0	1	310	−21	7
6	0	False	0	1	310	−20	10
7	0	False	0	1	310	−19	8
8	0	False	0	1	310	−15	6
9	0	False	0	1	310	−14	6
10	0	False	0	1	310	−11	8
11	0	False	0	1	310	−10	5
12	0	False	0	1	310	−9	5
13	0	False	0	1	310	−8	6
14	0	False	0	1	310	−6	4
15	0	False	0	1	310	−5	4
16	0	False	0	1	310	−4	5
17	0	False	0	1	310	−3	3
18	0	False	0	1	310	−2	3
19	0	False	0	1	310	−1	2
20	0	False	0	1	310	0	1

Column E adds the win or loss in Column D to the previous value in Column E, creating a running total of the loss and eventual win.

Column F, just for convenience converts the units won or lost to dollars.

USE

This model can show you very quickly the good and bad points of the martingale. Since it randomly generates wins and losses, all you need to do to see another scenario is hit your Calculate Now command

(CMD =). Once you've become familiar with the base case of 50% winning probability and $1:$1 win to loss size, see what's important in managing a martingale by tweaking the probability of winning and the ratio of wins to losses.

For some analytical adventure, turn the win/loss ratio into a random variable mapped between 1 and 5 and skewed to the left between 1 and 3, a pretty typical trading situation.

Appendix J

APPLYING MARTINGALES TO TRADING CAMPAIGNS

This appendix gives Excel code to allow comparison of the equity curves for a trading combination with a simple MAE stop and the same combination with a martingale applied to it. The equity curves that result from this analysis can be converted to returns series and analyzed for volatility and risk/reward ratios. Plotted as they stand, though, they produce an excellent visual comparison which most will find almost fully informative.

This example is set up slightly differently than those in the earlier appendices. The first 64 rows are given over to the data itself in columns A through E. The columns, however, are the same as those arranged in Appendix F through Column I, the MAE computation. If you have this model haul it out and discard all columns after I, not forgetting to save the revised model under a different name.

Next go to cell F63 and enter, left to right the following titles in the columns as shown in Figure J–1.

Now, two initial values for these columns must be set. In cell J61 enter the value .31. Later you can change this to adjust the model to

	F	G	H	I	J	K	L	M	N	O
	T					Number	Martingale's		Trend &	
	r					Blocks	Blocks	Martingale	Martingale	
	a				Trend	Won or	Outstanding	Equity	Equity	
	d					Lost				
63	e	Position	Trend P&L	MAE	Equity					Margin
64	1	-31.04	FALSE	FALSE	0	FALSE	FALSE	FALSE	0	200
65	1	-31.04	FALSE	0	0	FALSE	FALSE	FALSE	0	200
66	1	-31.04	FALSE	0	0	FALSE	FALSE	FALSE	0	200
67	0	0	0.09	0.01	0.09	FALSE	FALSE	FALSE	0.09	FALSE

Figure J–1 Headings for Martingale Analysis. The model's first five columns and 63 rows are given over to data to feed the trading rules. Titles for the analysis are in cells F63:O63.

	Q	R
62	Bet Table	
63	-196	30
64	-166	27
65	-115	24
66	-94	21
67	-77	16
68	-76	18
69	-65	12
70	-61	15
71	-55	11
72	-54	11
73	-53	12
74	-45	10
75	-44	10
76	-43	11
77	-36	9
78	-32	11
79	-28	8
80	-27	8
81	-21	7
82	-20	7
83	-19	8
84	-15	6
85	-14	6
86	-11	8
87	-10	5
88	-9	5
89	-8	6
90	-6	4
91	-5	4
92	-4	5
93	-3	3
94	-2	3
95	-1	2
96	0	1

Figure J–2 Bet Table for Crude. Equipped to handle adverse runs up to twelve losses and 23-trade martingales, the Crude bet table is much longer than the simulation's bet table in Appendix I.

your needs. In cell O59 enter the title "Margin in $"; in O60, enter $2000; and in O61, enter the formula " = O59/10" without the quotes. This assumes your tradable trades at $10 per tick. Adjust as necessary to compute margin in trading points.

One other preparation is necessary before filling in the formulations for the day-to-day computations. That is to create the "Bet Table" as in Appendix I. This table must be filled in manually because its values are specific to the martingale I used. I began it at cell Q62 with the title "Bet Table." Enter it into the cells Q62:R96 as shown in Figure J–2.

This table is so much larger than that of the simulation model because Crude goes on longer runs!

Before leaving the bet table it must be defined to Excel. Highlight Q63:R96 and then select from the menu bar FORMULA/DEFINE NAME . . . Enter the name "Bet_Table" (without the quotes) and click OK. From now on, the model can refer to this entire table by the name we've just given it.

Next, move to the following cells and fill in the formulations specified:

Cell	Formulation
F64	=IF(E64>E52,IF(E64>E4,1,0),IF(E64<E4,-1,0))
G64	=IF(F63< >F64,IF(F64=1,-E64,IF(F64=-1,E64,0)),G63)
H64	FALSE
I64	FALSE
J64	0
K64	=IF(H64< >FALSE,IF(H64<0,IF(K63=FALSE,-1, -VLOOKUP(L63,BET_Table,2)),IF(K63 =FALSE,FALSE,VLOOKUP(L63,Bet_Table,2))),IF(L63> =0,FALSE,IF(M63>=0,FALSE,K63)))
L64	=IF(K64=FALSE,FALSE,IF(H64< >FALSE,K64 +L63,L63))
M64	=IF(L64=FALSE,FALSE,IF(H64<0,IF(J$61>I64, -H64*K64+M63,J$61*K64+M63),H64*K64+M63))
N640	
O64	=IF(G64< >0,IF(K64<0,O$61-K64*O$61,O$61 +K64*O$61),FALSE)

H64, I64, J64, and N64 all held initial values but, for the rest of the rows need formulas. To avoid typing row 65 again select F64:O65 and hit CMD-D. This will fill in row 65 with the formulas from 64 plus some initial values which you'll now overwrite with specific formulas. Enter the following formulas in the cells indicated.

Cell	Formulation
H65	=IF(G65< >G64,IF(G64>0,G64−E65,IF(G64<0,G64+E65)))
I65	=IF($G65< >0,IF($G64< >0,IF($H64=FALSE,IF ($G64<0,MAX(0,−$G64−$D65,$I64),MAX(0,$C65 −$G64,$I64)),IF($G64<0,MAX(0,−$G64 −$D65),MAX(0,$C65−$G64)))),IF($H65< > FALSE,IF($G64<0,MAX(0,−$G64 −$D65,$I64),MAX(0,$C65−$G64,$I64))))
J65	=IF($H65< >FALSE,IF(J$61<$I65,J64−J$61,J64 +$H65),J64)
N65	=IF(H65=FALSE,N64,IF(M65=FALSE,N64+J65 −J64,M65−M64+N64))

Wow! Seeing the actual logic behind "simple" trading ideas is astonishing!

Now, checking to see the last row of your data, (let's say row 3000, for example) select F65:O3000.* Then hit CMD-D. Excel may complain that the selection is too large to do with an Undo, but hit OK. Once it has copied itself, select Calculate Now (if you don't have Automatic Calculation turned on) and your equity curves are deposited in columns J and N.

With the various charting sequences in various packages of Excel, I forbear instructing on creating a chart but the most foolproof way is to make line charts your default chart type, select and move the two columns adjacent to each other, select the range you wish to chart and invoke the chart wizard. In Excel 4.0 for the Mac, the last efficient version of Excel, hit CMD-N, C, and return. Voila!

---

* An easy way to do this is put your cursor in cell F65, select GO TO and enter O3000 in the popup box. BEFORE you close the box, hold the shift key down and click OK. The entire area will be selected for you.

EXPLANATION

Columns F through I have already been explained in earlier Appendices. The Trade column computes whether a dual-moving average trade is on or off and in what direction. You can change this formulation to use the model for different trading rules. Column G computes and holds the position's entry price, negative (for cash outflow) for longs and positive for shorts. When the trade ends Column H computes the win or loss. Column I computes the maximum adverse excursion on each day of the trade and its final value.

Column J keeps a running total of the wins and losses, subject to the .31 MAE stop, resulting in the equity curve of the trading combination. Each time there is a closure of a trade, Column J checks to see if the adverse excursion exceeded the .31 level. If so, the trade is marked a loss of .31 even if it was a winning trade originally. This accounts for the negative impact of MAE—or any—stop.

To get to the martingale's equity curve, Column K waits until a losing trade is recorded. Then it computes the number of contracts or share blocks that were risked on the trade in units. These are the numbers used to track the martingale's sequence. Later as the martingale proceeds through more losses, it recomputes the number of contracts to be risked by looking up the values in the Bet Table. Using the bet table is preferable to encoding the elaborate martingale logic within the limitations of Excel. The bet table holds valid amounts to risk for the most common values in the martingale used here. If you want to experiment with a different martingale, you'll need to make the Excel logic or create a similar table by going through various win/loss sequences.

Column L is a running total of the contracts or share blocks that have been won or lost. If this running total turns to zero or positive the martingale is ended. Similarly, Column M keeps a running total of the trading points gained or lost during the progression of the martingale. If this turns positive the martingale is ended, placing the trader at a new high level of profitability.

Column N keeps a running total of the equity from the trend trade as impacted by the Martingale's results, in trading points. Winning and losing trend trades plus all the wins and losses of the martingale are summed here to create the martingale's equity curve.

Lastly, Column O computes from the number of blocks being traded in Column K the margin outstanding to support the Martingale. The per contract margin is taken from cell O61 where it can be adjusted to reflect your tradable.

Though it would take some expertise with Excel to modify the trading rules, it should be fairly easy for different date to be cut and pasted into the first five columns. Remembering, then, to adjust the stop value in J61 and the margin in points in O61, the model should be ready to serve in seeing the martingale's impact.

INDEX

Printed in the United States
91687LV00007B/27/A